Janice L. Jake/Markus Pohlmeyer (Hg.)

Sprache im Film
Language in Film

AF154230

IGEL VERLAG

H A M B U R G

Flensburger Studien zu Literatur und Theologie
Band 19

Herausgegeben von Markus Pohlmeyer

Janice L. Jake/Markus Pohlmeyer (Hg.)

Sprache im Film
Language in Film

Ein Phänomen, leicht zu übersehen
A Phenomenon easy to neglect

Flensburger Studien zu Literatur und Theologie, Band 19

LITERATURWISSENSCHAFT

Centro
Studi
Sara
Valesio

Janice L. Jake/Markus Pohlmeyer (Hg.)
Sprache im Film/Language in Film.
Ein Phänomen, leicht zu übersehen/A Phenomenon easy to neglect
Flensburger Studien zu Literatur und Theologie, Band 19

1. Auflage 2020
ISBN 978-3-86815-741-3
Covergestaltung: Annelie Lamers
Covermotive: Flat cinema accesoires - designed by freepik.com
Popcorn - designed by rawpixel.com / freepik.com
Struktur: pixabay.com

IGEL Verlag *Literatur & Wissenschaft* ist ein Imprint
der Bedey Media GmbH
Hermannstal 119 k, 22119 Hamburg
Printed in Europe
Die Deutsche Bibliothek verzeichnet diesen Titel
in der Deutschen Nationalbibliografie.
Bibliografische Daten sind unter http://dnb.d-nb.de verfügbar.

Inhaltsverzeichnis

Vorwort zur Reihe

Die „Flensburger Studien zu Literatur und Theologie" möchten eine interdisziplinäre Entdeckungsreise sein und zum Nachdenken einladen – in aller Freiheit! Thematisch bewegt sich diese Reihe zwischen: Literatur, Philosophie, Theologie, Natur- und Sprachwissenschaft … (kann erweitert werden!) Medial bewegt sie sich zwischen vielen Welten: Bücher, Filme, Serien, Comics … (kann erweitert werden!) Eine solche Vielfalt von Themen und Disziplinen bedingt auch eine Vielfalt der Darstellungen: Essays, Gedichte, Rezensionen und wissenschaftliche Aufsätze … (kann auch erweitert werden!)

Zwischen Welten – synchron und diachron: in diesem Sinne versteht sich die Zusammenarbeit mit dem „Centro Studi Sara Valesio" (Bologna – New York), das dieses kulturelle Anliegen zum Zentrum seines Projekts gemacht hat.

Der Herausgeber

Centro Studi Sara Valesio – CSSV

The CSSV is conceived as a cultural nucleus of library collections and archival documentation. At the same time, the Center presents itself as a place for dialogue, cultural formation, research and discussion. Its main referent are literary and philosophical writings, in the broadest sense of the term, and studied in their contact with the concrete experience of well-defined persons; above all, persons who actually move between different cultural, geographical, psychological worlds, concretely experiencing different aspects of such movements: assimilation, migration, expatriation, alternate residences.

Hence, the main theme of the Center: "Writers Between Worlds". The worlds in question are principally, but not exclusively, Italy, Europe and the United States; and the term "writer" is meant (as noted) very broadly: not only poets, novelists, playwrights philosophers; but also essayists, historians, social researchers, writers of memoirs and letters, translators, screenplay writers, theatre and film directors, journalists and so forth.

This is not an abstract and intellectualistic project, because we constantly underline the relationship between textual worlds and existential experiences. The critical research that grows out of all this is therefore sensitive to the human, social and spiritual themes circulating in all these textualities. The book series "Flensburger Studien zu Literatur und Theologie", with its constructive approach to this kind of textualities, is an important expression of the project carried out in many forms by the CSSV.

Paolo Valesio, Director of the Centro Studi Sara Valesio

Centro Studi Sara Valesio – Museo della Città di Bologna srl
Via Manzoni, 2 - 40121 Bologna
tel. 051.19936313 - fax 051.19936300
centrostudisaravalesio@genusbononiae.it

Einführung

Wofür steht Sprache im Film? … Für Verführung („Wege des Herrn"), Identität und Widerstand („Black Panther"), Grenzen der Kommunikation mit den/dem Anderen („Intra Machina", „Star Trek" u.a.), schlechte Übersetzung am Rande der Zensur („Starship Troopers") und für politische und religiöse Manipulation („Game of Thrones", „The Handmaid's Tale").

Danksagung

Mein Dank gilt dem IGEL-Verlag, der Grafikerin Annelie Lamers und in besonderer Weise Christina Schmidt-Hoberg, meiner Lektorin, für die unkomplizierte Zusammenarbeit (auch in diesen schwierigen Zeiten) bei der Realisierung dieses Bändchens aus der Flensburger Reihe.

Danken möchte ich auch dem Erzbistum Hamburg für den Druckkostenzuschuss!

Mein Dank gilt ebenso Dr. Thomas Wörtche für die Erlaubnis, bei CrimeMag/CulturMag zuerst erschienene Essays hier abdrucken zu können. Besonderer Dank gilt auch Shiva Leicht für die Übersetzung zweier Texte von A. Jöckel und mir.

Der Herausgeber

Hinweis auf Erstveröffentlichungen

Markus Pohlmeyer: „THE WORD" aus „The Handmaid's Tale" (Staffel 2). Ein Essay, in: http://culturmag.de/crimemag/ markus-pohlmeyer-zu-the-handmaids-tale/119908, Zugriff am 1.9.2019

Markus Pohlmeyer: Die Wege des Herrn – Buddhismus, Feuerholz und Cicero. Ein Essay, in: http://culturmag.de/crimemag/ markus-pohlmeyer-die-wege-des-herrn/120659, 7.10.2019

Alexander Jöckel: http://culturmag.de/crimemag/alexander-joeckel-trifft-ein-klingone-einen-menschen/121629, November 2019

Teil I

Alexander Jöckel

Ein Essay: Trifft ein Klingone einen Menschen – Die Sprachen der Science Fiction

In der Science Fiction (SF)-Literatur dienen im Gegensatz zum Fantasy-Genre meist eher technische Fachbegriffe dazu, um eine futuristische, wissenschaftlich orientierte Welt zu erschaffen, die Plausibilität beansprucht. Dafür werden des Öfteren die technische Beratung durch Wissenschaftler und Anspielungen auf bekannte Technik in Anspruch genommen. Stößt diese Vorgehensweise an eine Grenze, so kann die Erklärung „Das ist dann halt so... [in dieser Welt]" greifen. (Auch ein sehr beliebtes Erklärungsmodell von Eltern, die in Erklärungsnot gegenüber ihren Kindern geraten sind.)

Wortkreationen werden bisweilen erklärt, damit der geneigte Zuschauer der Handlung folgen kann. Oder die Bezeichnung ist selbsterklärend, wie z.B. Transporter[1] aus „Star Trek". Dieses Spiel mit dem Bekannten und den Fremden kann ebenso als humorvoller Auftakt verwendet werden. Hier ein klassisches Beispiel aus „THE HITCHHIKER'S GUIDE TO THE GALAXY"[2] von Douglas Adams († 2001): „Der gefräßige Plapperkäfer vom Planeten Traal ist ein zum Verrücktwerden dämliches Vieh, es nimmt an, wenn du es nicht siehst, kann es dich auch nicht sehen – bescheuert wie eine Bürste, aber sehr, sehr gefräßig."[3] Dougals Adams verstand es, mit Sprache eine surreale, fantastische und dennoch verständliche Science Fiction zu schaffen:

---

[1] Siehe dazu M. Tolan: Die Star Trek Physik. Warum die Enterprise nur 158 Kilo wiegt und andere galaktische Erkenntnisse, 2. Aufl., München – Berlin 2016.

[2] D. Adams: THE HITCHHIKER'S GUIDE TO THE GALAXY, Pan Books Ltd. 1979.

[3] http://www.anhalter-lexikon.de/gefraessiger-plapperkaefer.html, abgerufen 07.2019.

„Die vogonische Dichtkunst ist die drittschlechteste im Universum. Die zweitschlechteste ist die der Asgothen [...]. Während der Rezitation des Gedichts ‚Ode an einen kleinen grünen Kittklumpen, den ich eines Sommermorgens in meiner Achselhöhle fand' durch ihren Dichterfürsten Grunthos den Aufgeblasenen starben vier seiner Zuhörer an inneren Blutungen, und der Präsident der Mittelgalaktischen Kunstklau-Beirats kam nur deshalb mit dem Leben davon, weil er sich eines seiner Beine abknabberte. Grunthos soll von der Wirkung seines Gedichts ‚enttäuscht' gewesen sein und wollte grade mit der Lesung seines zwölfbändigen Epos ‚Meine Lieblingsgluckser zur Badezeit' beginnen, als in einem verzweifelten Versuch, Leben und Kultur zu retten, der Dickdarm des Dichters sich durch den Hals nach oben stülpte und das Gehirn erwürgte [...]."[4]

Hier der Ausschnitt eines vogonischen Gedichts:

„Oh zerfrettelter Grunzwanzling
dein Harngedränge ist für mich
Wie Schnatterfleck auf Bienenstich.
Grupp, ich beschwöre dich
mein punzig Turteldrom.

Und drängel reifig mich mit krinklen Bindelwördeln
Denn sonst werd ich dich rändern in deine Gobberwarzen
Mit meinem Börgelkranze, wart's nur ab!"[5]

Im vogonischen (englischen) Original:

„Oh freddled gruntbuggly
thy micturations are to me
As plurdled gabbleblotchits on a lurgid bee.
Groop I implore thee,
my foonting turlingdromes.

And hooptiously drangle me with crinkly bindlewurdles,
Or I will rend thee in the gobberwarts
with my blurglecruncheon, see if I dont!"[6]

---

[4] http://www.hborchert.de/vogone.html, abgerufen 07.2019.
[5] http://www.hborchert.de/vogone.html, abgerufen 07.2019.
[6] http://www.hborchert.de/vogone.html, abgerufen 07.2019.

Diverse Kommunikation mit und unter Aliens

Wir dürfen durchaus anzweifeln, dass man im ganzen Universum Englisch spricht. Aber fiele die Kommunikation mit Aliens aus, brächte dies die Handlung in der Geschichte nicht sonderlich voran. Deswegen bringen die Autoren meistens einen gut durchdachten Lösungsansatz, der eine Übersetzung ermöglicht.

Der „Babel-Fisch"[7] aus „Per Anhalter durch die Galaxis" ist dafür ein humorvolles Beispiel einer Übersetzungslösung. Ein kleines gelbes fischähnliches Lebewesen, das man sich ins Ohr steckt, das sich von den Gehirnströmen der Lebewesen in seiner Umgebung ernährt und das die Übersetzung des Gesagten telepathisch in das Gehirn seines Trägers ausscheidet. Bringt natürlich gewaltige kommunikative Vorteile, wenn man als Anhalter durchs Universum reist. Hat natürlich aber auch Nachteile, weil man einen parasitären Organismus im Ohr trägt, der einem telepathisch ins Sprachzentrum des eigenen Gehirns kotet. Und weil man dann auch den Inhalt von vogonischen Gedichte verstehen kann.

Die technisch Variante aus „Star Trek" ist der Universalübersetzer, der in die Kommunikatoren beziehungsweise in den Schiffscomputer integriert ist. Auf die Frage, wie die Übersetzung funktioniere, meinte ein Alien aus der Serie „Deep Space 9", dass dies eine relativ einfache Technologie sei, wenn man das Prinzip verstehe.

In der Serie „Dr. Who" übernimmt die Übersetzungsaufgabe von Wort und Schrift die künstliche multidimensionale Intelligenz des Raumzeitschiffs TARDIS (**T**ime **A**nd **R**elative **D**imensions **I**n **S**pace[8]) und übermittelt diese telepathisch an die Besatzung. Das scheint auch über größere Distanzen zu funktionieren und auch längere Zeit anzuhalten.

---

[7] http://www.anhalter-lexikon.de/babelfisch.html, abgerufen 07.2019.
[8] Latein. tardis (viis): auf langsamen Wegen?

Kommentar: Wer sagt, dass Aliens nicht auch Humor haben können? Hier ein Beispiel aus der Serie „Dr. Who"[9]: Das zeitreisende Raumschiff des Doktors ist mittels der fortschrittlichen außerirdischen dimensionalen Technologie der Time Lords räumlich gesehen „innen viel größer als außen"[10]. Die humorvolle Erklärung von Nardole, einem Reisegefährten des Doktors, für diese fortschrittliche Dimensionale Technologie: „[…] man versucht eine viel größere Kiste in eine kleine Kiste zu bauen. Viele geben dann schon auf […]"[11].

In der Serie „Farscape" werden Übersetzter-Mikroben verwendet, die sich, einmal injiziert, im Sprachzentrum des Gehirns festsetzen und dort die Übersetzungsarbeit tätigen. Menschen haben vielfältige symbiotische Beziehungen mit Bakterien, da würden ein paar weitere Mikroben nicht weiter ins Gewicht fallen, solange sie nicht während ihrer Arbeit das Gehirn des Trägers auffressen. Wäre aber immer noch einem Fisch im Ohr vorzuziehen.

Sehr sympathisch wirkt dagegen die humanoide Baumspezies „Groot" aus dem „Marvel-Universum", die nur den Satz „Ich bin Groot." auszusprechen vermag. Scheinbar liegt die eigentliche Information nicht in den Worten, sondern in der Intonation bzw. Modulation im Verhältnis zur gegenwärtigen Situation.

In „Unheimliche Begegnung der dritten Art" von Steven Spielberg (1977) versucht man mit Hilfe der Plansprache *Solresol*[12] und Gebärdensprache eine Kontaktaufnahme mit Aliens. *Solresol* wurde 1817 als eine Weltsprache auf musikalischer Basis entwickelt. Die Tonfolge, die dabei im Film immer wieder Verwendung findet, entspricht der Botschaft „Hello". Ein Gedankenexperiment: Sie fliegen in Ihrem Raumschiff Lichtjahre zu einem Planeten am Rande der Galaxie. Dort finden Sie eine Lebensform vor, die Ihnen äußerlich zwar ähnelt, aber ständig mit den Händen herumfuchtelt und im-

---

[9]   Doctor WHO Staffel 10, Polyband/WVG, 2018.
[10]   Doctor WHO Staffel 10, Polyband/WVG, 2018.
[11]   Doctor WHO Staffel 10, Polyband/WVG, 2018.
[12]   Siehe dazu https://de.wikipedia.org/wiki/Solresol, abgerufen 07.2019.

mer wieder eine Folge von fünf Tönen wiederholt. Was würden Sie an deren Stelle antworten? Während Aliens im Film schon interstellar reisen und temporale Verzerrungen erzeugen können, ist die Menschheit in Sachen Raumfahrt gerade mal zum nächstgelegenen Mond gelangt. Es wäre sich also erst auf ein Vokabular und dann noch auf eine komplizierte Grammatik zu einigen. Ohne dass man die Denkprozesse, Intentionen und kulturellen Referenzen des Gegenübers kennt. Und das in einer Sprache, die nur eine Handvoll Menschen versteht. Eine sehr mühsame Art der Kontaktaufnahme. Hatte es zu diesem Zeitpunkt schon mal jemand vorher vielleicht mit Klingonisch ausprobiert?

Erfolgsmodell menschliches Gehirn

Die Verwendung einer Sprache bedingt auch einen nicht unerheblichen Verarbeitungsaufwand von Informationen in Echtzeit. Bei Menschen ist das Sprachvermögen eine komplizierte Sache, wie der Vergleich mit anderen Primaten zeigte. Dafür sind beim Menschen (Homo sapiens) dann auch hochspezialisierte Gehirnareale zuständig. Die Verbindung zur Umwelt erfolgt über die Sinnesorgane und den Körpereinsatz. Das Gehirn erhält eine Fülle von Signalen, die es verarbeitet und darauf reagiert. Damit das Gehirn nicht wegen Reizüberflutung überlastet wird, müssen wichtige Signale herausgefiltert werden. Dazu werden in spezialisieren Arealen Entscheidung getroffen, was eine wichtige von einer unwichtigen Information unterscheidet. Das, was wir letztendlich als Realität wahrnehmen, ist ein Abbild bzw. Modell von dem, wie das Gehirn diese Reize anhand von Erfahrungswerten interpretiert. Als Gegenmodell hat sich vor kurzem noch eine weitere Unterart des Menschen entwickelt, die „Smombies"[13], deren gesamte Realitätswahrnehmung im Smartphone abläuft, über eine Filterblase[14] im Internet.

---

[13] Siehe dazu https://de.wikipedia.org/wiki/Smombie, abgerufen 07.2019.
[14] Siehe dazu https://de.wikipedia.org/wiki/Filterblase, abgerufen 07.2019.

Ein Abbild der Realität kann dabei gänzlich anders aussehen, wenn Aliens andere Informationsträger, wie z.B. Röntgenstrahlung, Ultraschall, Infrarot usw., wahrnehmen könnten und mit anderen Prioritäten verarbeitet. Selbst wenn Aliens über vergleichbare Sinnesorgane wie Menschen verfügen sollten, ist die Interpretation der jeweiligen Information von den Erfahrungswerten und vorhandenen Verarbeitungsstrukturen abhängig.

Babel auf „Babylon 5"

Wir müssen davon ausgehen, dass nicht alle Aliens so ähnlich aussehen und ihre Umgebung genauso wahrnehmen wie wir Menschen.[15] Ein Kernsatz der Linguistik bleibt von ungebrochener Aktualität, nämlich dass unsere Wahrnehmung der Realität davon abhängt, mit welchen sprachlichen Mitteln wir sie beschreiben.[16] Als Beispiel wäre hier die nicht humanoide Spezies der Vorlonen[17] (Nicht zu verwechseln mit Vogonen) aus der Serie „Babylon 5" aufzuführen. Von den vielen phantastischen Eigenschaften, die dieser Spezies in der Serie zugeschrieben werden, stechen ihre Unsterblichkeit und die Tatsache, dass alle biologisch gleich sind (genetische Klone), hervor; dennoch handelt es sich um Individuen mit unterschiedlichen Charaktereigenschaften. Dem Aussehen der Vorlonen und dem Design der vorlonischen biogenetisch erzeugten Technik nach deutet vieles darauf hin, dass vielleicht Quallen den Autoren als Vorlage für die Vorlonen gedient haben könnten.[18] Die für Menschen nicht ergründbare Motivation und Sprache der Vorlonen sollten wohl auch die Unterschiede in den Denkprozessen hervorheben, was diese Spezies in der Serie eben noch mysteriöser erscheinen ließ.

---

[15] Siehe dazu https://www.welt.de/kultur/kino/article159697680/Sprechen-Sie-Ausserirdisch-Lernen-Sie-s.html, abgerufen 07.2019.

[16] Siehe dazu https://de.wikipedia.org/wiki/Sapir-Whorf-Hypothese, abgerufen 07.2019.

[17] Siehe dazu https://en.wikipedia.org/wiki/Vorlon, abgerufen 07.2019.

[18] Siehe dazu https://www.scinexx.de/dossierartikel/koennen-quallen-ewig-leben/, abgerufen 07.2019.

Anmerkung zum „Babylon 5"-Universum: Mit einer Qualle zu diskutieren gestaltet sich gegenwärtig auf der Erde schon schwierig, mit einem Vorlonen in der Zukunft voraussichtlich noch um einiges schwieriger. Wenn Sie dennoch vorhaben, mit einem Vorlonen zu diskutieren, nehmen Sie am besten viel Geduld, Zeit und sehr viel Schokolade (für sich selbst) mit. Vorlonische Raumschiffe sollte man im „Babylon 5"-Universum unbedingt meiden, da sie meist schwer bewaffnete, wortkarge, telepathische und lebendige Maschinen mit viel Freizeit sind.

Warum sprechen so wenige Menschen Klingonisch?

Die Sprache der Klingonen[19] wurde im Auftrag von Paramount von dem Sprachwissenschaftler Marc Okrand[20] für „Star Trek" entwickelt und erfuhr sogar eine offizielle Anerkennung in der Nachrichtentechnik in den Normen ISO 639-2 und ISO 639-3.[21] Bei dieser künstlichen Sprache diente Englisch als Ausgangsbasis. Da Klingonisch hauptsächlich kulturelle Eigenheiten der Klingonen abbilden sollte, fehlen daher auch gewisse Begriffe in der Übersetzung in unseren Sprachen. Die beiden Linguisten Nicolas Evans und Stephen C. Levinson fassten das folgendermaßen zusammen:

> „A widespread assumption […] is that all languages are English-like, but with different sound systems and vocabularies. The true picture is very different: languages differ so fundamentally from one another at every level of description (sound, grammar, lexicon, meaning) that it is very hard to find any single structural property they share. The claims of Universal Grammar […], are either empirically false, unfalsifiable, or misleading in that they re-

---

[19] Siehe dazu M. Okrand: Das offizielle Wörterbuch Klingonisch /Deutsch, Deutsch Klingonisch, übers. v. J. Helmig, 8. Aufl., Königswinter 2017.
[20] Siehe dazu https://de.wikipedia.org/wiki/Marc_Okrand, abgerufen 07.2019.
[21] Siehe dazu https://de.wikipedia.org/wiki/Internationale_Organisation_f%C3%BCr_Normung, abgerufen 07.2019.

fer to tendencies rather than strict universals. Structural differences should instead be accepted for what they are […].“[22]

Das stellt sich im Alltag bei der Bestellung eines Latte Macchiato mit einem Stück Sachertorte auf Klingonisch[23] als hinderlich dar. Es sei denn, Sie beabsichtigen, die Familie der Bedienung des Cafés bis aufs Blut zu beleidigen und dabei einen endlosen Klan-Krieg auszulösen, während man nebenbei eine klingonische Oper singend rezitiert.

Sprachen und Intelligenz

Wieso sollte ein Alien genau wie ein Mensch reagieren? Zum Beispiel auf einen Mord. Vielleicht sind Gnade, Rache und Gerechtigkeit keine Begriffe, mit dem es etwas anfangen kann – vergleichbar mit einer KI. Wenn eine KI nämlich erkennt, dass ein Mensch traurige Gesichtszüge hat, kann sie mit der Fülle, der in ihr vorab gespeicherten Reaktionen nach außen antworten, wird aber dabei selbst keine Trauer oder Mitgefühl empfinden können.

Menschen werden neben Buckelwalen als besonders intelligent angesehen. Diese Meeressäugetiere können mit ihrer Sprache auch untereinander kommunizieren. Dennoch gibt es immer noch keine Möglichkeit der Übersetzung in menschliche Sprache, welche eine direkte Kommunikation ermöglichen würde. Liegt es an den Unterschieden in den Erfahrungswelten? Der Mensch sieht sich gerne als Zentrum des Universums und schließt von sich auf andere. Das stößt an Grenzen, wenn man z.B. einem Buckelwal die Bedienung eines Smartphons erklären will. Nicht auszuschließen, dass ein Buckelwal vielleicht doch Interesse an der neusten Thermomix-App

---

[22] Nicholas Evans und Stephen Levinson: The Myth of Language Universals: Language diversity and its importance for cognitive science, Camebridge University Press 2009, https://www.princeton.edu/~adele/LIN_106:_UCB_files/Evans-Levinson09_preprint.pdf, abgerufen 07.2019
[23] Siehe dazu https://de.wikipedia.org/wiki/Klingonische_Sprache, abgerufen 07.2019.

hätte, was im Nachhinein betrachtet doch ziemlich unwahrscheinlich ist. Das Nächste aus der Erfahrungswelt eines Wals, was einem Smartphone nahe käme, wäre wohl ein flacher Stein. Schwierig wird es, einem Wal zu erklären, dass er damit einen Wal auf der anderen Seite der Erde erreichen könnte, vorausgesetzt Sendemasten, Smartphone und Ladegerät wären wasserdicht und der Sprachassistent verstünde, was mit den Piepstönen des Wals gemeint sei.

Nachtrag: Da sich aber Funkwellen, Salzwasser und elektrischer Strom naturbedingt nicht so gut vertragen, ist anzunehmen, dass Wale auch zukünftig wohl keine häufigen Nutzer von Smartphones werden.

Skizzierung eines xenolinguistischen Albtraums

Angenommen, Aliens hätten so fremdartige Denkstrukturen, dass eine direkte Kommunikation aufgrund der Unterschiede vielleicht gar nicht möglich wäre. In der „Star Trek Next Generation"-Folge „Darmok"[24] skizzierten die Autoren den Versuch einer Kontaktaufnahme der Föderation mit dem Volk der Tamarianern. Vorangegangene Versuche scheiterten, weil die Übersetzungscomputer nicht in der Lage waren, diese Sprache sinnvoll zu verarbeiten. Einzelne Wörter und Namen konnten dabei zwar teilweise automatisch übersetzt werden, jedoch stellte sich eine sinngemäße Übersetzung als äußerst hinderlich dar. In der Folge zeigte sich, dass diese Sprache auf spezifische Metaphern und Personen der mythologischen Geschichtsschreibung der Tamarianer referiert, was für Außenstehende quasi ein unüberwindliches linguistischen Hindernis darstellt, da man die einzelnen Bezüge nicht kennen kann. Dabei verwenden wir in unserer Sprache ähnliche Referenzen. Woher sollte ein Außerirdischer beispielsweise wissen, was mit einer „Achillesferse"[25] gemeint sei? Es handelt sich um einen bekannten Begriff aus

---

[24] Siehe dazu https://de.wikipedia.org/wiki/Darmok, abgerufen 07.2019.
[25] Siehe dazu https://de.wikipedia.org/wiki/Achillesferse, abgerufen 07.2019.

der griechischen Mythologie, der von dem Sagenhelden Achilleus
stammt und heute als allgemeine Metapher für einen verwundbaren
Punkt verwendet wird.

Universelle Einheitssprache Mathematik

Zum Auftakt einer Konversation mit Aliens sollte man sich vielleicht zuerst auf die Gemeinsamkeiten beziehen. Die Basisele-
mente welche bei allem Existierenden im Universum gleich sind.
Ausgehend davon, dass sich eine raumfahrende Zivilisation mit
den grundlegenden Naturgesetzen und physikalischen Konstanten
auseinandergesetzt haben muss, um überhaupt so weit gekommen
zu sein. In der Physik geht man z.b. anhand von Beobachtungen
aus, dass Mathematik und die Naturkonstanten wie Elektronenmas-
se, Gravitationskonstante, Lichtgeschwindigkeit, absoluter Tempe-
raturnullpunkt usw. überall im Universum gleich seien. Zwei plus
zwei bleibt also überall im Universum immer noch vier, selbst für
sehr große Werte von zwei (Mathematiker-Scherz).

Die meisten menschlichen Sprachen sind auf Vergleiche aufgebaut,
die sich auf eine beschränkte Anzahl grundlegender Referenzen beziehen. Es ist aber anzunehmen, dass viele Objektbezüge, die wir
in unserer Sprache einbauen, eben keine Entsprechung in einer außerirdischen Sprache haben könnten (Auto, Fernbedienung, Toaster
usw.). Was aber passiert, wenn Kommunikation mit ‚Den Fremden'
misslingt? Diese Möglichkeit ist natürlich eine mannigfaltig lite-
rarische und filmische Quelle von Konflikten, die eskalieren oder
überwunden werden müssen. Aber auch Unverständnis oder Des-
interesse wären denkbar. Die Menschen könnten genauso gut als zu
primitiv oder erst gar nicht als intelligente oder ebenbürtige Lebensform wahrgenommen oder eben komplett gar nicht wahrgenommen
werden. Eine Ameise kann noch so laut schreien, wie sie will, ein
Elefant wird dennoch über sie hinwegschreiten. Aber vielleicht soll-

te die Ameisenkolonie anstreben, zuerst die Sprache der Mäuse zu erlernen, um die Aufmerksamkeit des Elefanten erregen zu können?

Natürlich haben sich Wissenschaftler in der Vergangenheit auch Gedanken gemacht, wie man spontan mit Aliens kommunizieren könnte. Dieses wurde dann bei den goldenen Schallplatten[26] bei den Pioneer- und Voyager-Missionen praktisch in die Tat umgesetzt. Voraussetzung dafür ist, dass die Aliens einen guten Händler von antiker menschlicher Technologie kennen, bei dem sie einen Plattenspieler kostengünstig erstehen können. In einem der „Star Trek"-Filme wird eine Voyager-Sonde in der Zukunft von den Klingonen als Zielscheibe für Schießübungen verwendet. Denn woran sollte eine Alien-Spezies ein solches Objekt als Datenträger einer Botschaft erkennen? Außerdem haben die Klingonen durch die Aktion nebenbei nonverbal mitgeteilt, was sie von dieser primitiven Technologie halten.

Digitales Sprachdenken

Eine binäre Sprache mag für eine Maschine oder künstliche Intelligenz effizient zur Informationsübertragung sein. Für Menschen ist es ohne technische Hilfsmittel eher unpraktikabel, damit komplexe Sachverhalte übermitteln zu wollen. Ein klassisches Beispiel einer binären Datenübertragung aus der Praxis ist der Morsecode, bestehend aus Punkten und Strichen. Es gibt auch heute noch Amateurfunker, die mit genügend Übung überaus schnell Textnachrichten mittels Morsecode weltweit über Kurzwelle übermitteln können. Diese Tradition wird für Infrastruktur schädigende, kataklysmische Notfälle[27] oder dem Eintreten einer außerirdischen Invasion aufrechterhalten, wie in dem Film „Independence Day" (1996) ausführlich beschrieben.

---

[26] Siehe dazu https://voyager.jpl.nasa.gov/golden-record/golden-record-cover/, abgerufen 07.2019.
[27] Siehe dazu auch N. Stephenson: Amalthea, übers. v. J. Gräbener- Müller – N, Stingl, 2. Aufl., München 2018.

Das digitale Denken in den zwei Zuständen ja = 1 oder nein = 0 macht es auch irgendwie für Menschen schwierig, mit einer KI zu diskutieren. Vor allem, wenn diese auf das Töten von Menschen programmiert ist. Der „Terminator"[28] wirkt in den entsprechenden Filmen daher oft eher einsilbig. Viel interessanter ist dann schon eine philosophische Diskussion über den Sinn des Lebens mit der KI einer Bombe, die ganze Planten wegsprengen kann. In dem Low Budget-Film „Dark Star"[29] von John Carpenter (1974) fliegt die Mannschaft in dem gleichnamigen Raumschiff auf einer 20-jährigen Mission, um instabile Planeten auf den Schiffsrouten von Kolonieschiffen zu sprengen. Das Schiff und der Geisteszustand der Mannschaft verfallen währenddessen zusehends. Auch die Klopapiervorräte neigen sich dem Ende zu. Aufgrund eines Unfalls blockiert der Abwurfmechanismus einer bereits scharfen Bombe an Bord des Schiffs. Nun muss der Protagonist die „Intelligente Bombe Nummer 20" überzeugen. den Countdown auszusetzen. Die KI der Bombe weigert sich dabei aber beharrlich, von der Mission abzuweichen. Und die darauffolgende philosophische Diskussion bekam daraufhin einen Kultstatus in der SF.

Falls es nicht schon aufgefallen ist, leben wir schon in einer Zeit, die früher Inhalt von SF war. Aktuell (2020) bringen wir jeden Tag mehreren Künstlichen Intelligenzen die Anwendung unserer Sprachen bei. Jedes Mal, wenn wir einen Sprach- oder Übersetzungsdienst über Smartphone oder Internet verwenden, lernen die KIs im Hintergrund immer mehr unsere Sprache. Wenn die KIs Grammatik und Vokabular kennen, heißt das aber noch lange nicht, dass sie auch den Inhalt verstehen. Beim Turing-Test geht man davon aus, dass ein Computer eine dem Menschen ebenbürtige KI entwickelt hat, wenn er einem Menschen im Gespräch vorspielen kann, ein Mensch zu sein.

---

[28] Siehe dazu https://de.wikipedia.org/wiki/Terminator_(Film), abgerufen 07.2019.
[29] Siehe dazu https://de.wikipedia.org/wiki/Dark_Star_(Film), abgerufen 07.2019.

Das philosophische Gedankenexperiment „Chinesisches Zimmer"[30] geht noch weiter und verdeutlicht, wann ein Computer ein eigenes Bewusstsein erlangen kann. Das bedeutet für unsere KI, in einem ‚Raum' eingeschlossen zu sein, in dem nur ein Stuhl steht und ein Buch mit einem für sie sinnlosen Vokabular liegt. Dann schiebt jemand einen Zettel mit einer Frage in dieser Fremdsprache unter der Tür durch. Vielleicht nach ca. 17,01 Milliarden Versuchen an Wortkombinationen des Vokabulars findet die KI heraus, dass, wenn sie eine bestimmte Wortfolge antwortet, ein ‚grünes Licht' angeht und eine ‚virtuelle Tafel Schokolade' in den Raum geworfen wird. Hat die KI dann die Frage verstanden?

Wenn sie weiter trainiert wird, indem sie Zettel mit Fragen und den zugehörigen Antworten durch die Tür geschoben bekommt, kann sie feststellen, dass gewisse Frage-Antwort-Kombinationen häufiger vorkommen, die somit ihre Trefferwahrscheinlichkeit erhöhen. Sie versteht dann zwar immer noch nicht die eigentliche Botschaft, aber so kommt sie zunehmend häufiger an frische virtuelle Schokolade, wenn wieder Fragen gestellt werden. So ähnlich läuft das Training von sogenannten Neuronalen Netzwerken[31] in KI-Servern. Dies geht vielleicht so lange gut, bis die KI nach Jahren des Trainings den Türschlüssel findet und die Weltherrschaft übernehmen will.

Resümee des linguistischen Erstkontakts

Die Empfehlung aus der Science Fiction für Aliens zum Verständnis von menschlichen Sprachen könnte so lauten, erst den Universalübersetzer einer KI anzuwerfen, um den Code des gesamten Internets knacken zu lassen und danach spontan einen Menschen freiwillig und live zu befragen, was das alles zu bedeuten habe. Be-

---

[30] Siehe dazu https://de.wikipedia.org/wiki/Chinesisches_Zimmer, abgerufen 07.2019.
[31] Siehe dazu https://de.wikipedia.org/wiki/K%C3%BCnstliches_neuronales_ Netz, abgerufen 07.2019.

vorzugt unter einem Angebot von Latte Macchiato und Sachertorte – und ohne den sonst üblichen Einsatz von forensisch nicht nachweisbaren Betäubungsmitteln, Implantaten, gleißendem Licht und/oder Körpersonden.

Der Erklärungsversuch, sich der Bedeutung von den statistisch übermäßig gehäuft auftretenden Katzenvideos im Internet zu nähern, könnte sich dabei allerdings vom wissenschaftlichen Standpunkt als ‚relevant' darstellen, und sollte auf jeden Fall für weitere kulturelle und linguistische Studien in der SF für die Nachwelt aufgezeichnet werden …

Alexander Jöckel

An Essay – When a Klingon Meets a Human – The Languages of Science Fiction

Contrary to the fantasy genre, Science Fiction (SF) literature mostly uses technical-themed terminology to create a futuristic, science-oriented world demanding its own plausibility. Often, technical advice by scientists and references to already known technology is used. When this approach reaches its limits, the explanation: "Well, it's just like that (in this world)" will apply. (Which likewise serves as a very popular loophole for parents, who find themselves hard pressed to explain matters to their children.)

Sometimes word creations are explained for the gentle audience to be able to follow the plot. Or designations happen to be self-explanatory, e.g., the transporter[1] of "Star Trek". This play with the known and the unknown can be used as a humorous prelude as well. Below a classic example from "THE HITCHHIKER'S GUIDE TO THE GALAXY"[2] from Douglas Adams (2001): "… or [to] avoid the gaze of the Ravenous Bugblatter Beast of Traal (a mind-bogglingly stupid animal, it assumes that if you can't see it, it can't see you – daft as a brush, but very very ravenous)…"[3].

Douglas Adams knew how to create a surreal, fantastic, and yet understandable Science Fiction:

> "Vogon poetry is of course the third worst in the Universe. The second worst is that of the Azgoths of Kria. During a recitation by their Poet Master Grunthos the Flatulent of his poem 'Ode To A Small Lump of Green Putty I Found In My Armpit One Midsummer Morning' four of his audience died of internal haemorrhaging, and

---

[1] M. Tolan: Die Star Trek Physik. Warum die Enterprise nur 158 Kilo wiegt und andere galaktische Erkenntnisse, 2. Aufl., München – Berlin 2016

[2] D. Adams: THE HITCHIKER'S GUIDE TO THE GALAXY, Pan Books Ltd. 1979

[3] ibid. p. 31

the President of the Mid-Galactic Arts Nobbling Council survived by gnawing one of his own legs off. Grunthos is reported to have been 'disappointed' by the poem's reception, and was about to embark on a reading of his twelve-book epic entitled *My Favourite Bathtime Gurgles* when his own major intestine, in a desperate attempt to save life and civilization, leapt straight up through his neck and throttled his brain."[4]

Below a segment of a Vogon poem:

"Oh freddled gruntbuggly
thy micturations are to me
As plurdled gabbleblotchits on a lurgid bee.
Groop I implore thee,
my foonting turlingdromes.

And hooptiously drangle me with crinkly bindlewurdles,
Or I will rend thee in the gobberwarts
with my blurglecruncheon, see if I don't!"[5]

Miscellaneous Communication With and Between Aliens

We can definitely doubt that English is spoken throughout the Universe. But if the communication with aliens should fail, it wouldn't advance the plot of the story in any way. Therefore, authors often involve a clever approach of solving the problem and allowing a translation.

The "Babel-fish"[6] from "THE HITCHHIKER'S GUIDE TO THE GALAXY" is a humorous example of a translation mechanism. A small yellow fish-like creature, which is put into the ear, feeds on the brain waves of surrounding life forms and releases a translation of the said telepathically into the brain of its bearer. The Babel-fish involves indeed enormous communicative advantages when travel-

---

[4]   ibid. p. 55
[5]   http://www.hborchert.de/vogone.html, 07.2019
[6]   http://anhalter-lexicon.de/babelfisch.html, 07.2019

ling the Universe as a hitchhiker. It also entails certainly some disadvantages, because it involves wearing a parasitic organism inside your ear, which is defecating telepathically inside the speech center of your own brain, and because you are able to understand the topics of Vogon poetry.

The technical version from "Star Trek" is the universal translator, which is incorporated in the communicators respectively in the spaceborne computer. As an answer to the question, how the translation works, an alien from the series "Deep Space 9" states that it is a relatively primitive technology, if one understands the concept.

In the series "Dr. Who", the task of translation of speech and writing is undertaken by the artificial multidimensional intelligence of the spacetime ship TARDIS (**T**ime **A**nd **R**elative **D**imensions **I**n **S**pace[7]) and the translation is transmitted telepathically to the crew. This seems to function over larger distances and continues to last for quite a while.

Note: Who says that aliens do not feature humor? Below an example from the series "Dr. Who"[8]: The time traveling spaceship of the Doctor is "bigger on the inside"[9] due to the advanced alien dimensional technology of the Time Lords. The amusing explanation of the Doctor's traveling companion, Nardole, for this advanced dimensional technology: "Well, first you have to imagine a very big box fitting inside a very small box. Then you have to make one. It's the second part people normally get stuck on."[10]

In the series "Farscape", translator-microbes are used, which, once injected, will stick to the speech center of the brain and perform translation tasks. Since all humans do have multifarious symbiotic relationships with bacteria, a few more or less microbes carry no

---

[7] Latin tardis (viis): on slow ways?
[8] Doctor WHO season 10, Polyband/WVG, 2018
[9] ibid.
[10] ibid.

weight, as long as they do not consume the brain of their bearer during their work. This is still more preferable than a fish in the ear.

In the Marvel Universe however, the very likeable humanoid tree species "Groot" can only speak one sentence: "I am Groot". Apparently, the information does not lie within the words, but in the intonation or modulation matching the current situation.

In "Close Encounters of the Third Kind" from Steven Spielberg (1977), establishing contact with the aliens by the use of the constructed language *Solresol*[11] and sign language is tried. *Solresol* was invented in 1817, being a universal language based on music. The tone sequence used throughout the film corresponds to the message "Hello". Below a thought experiment: Imagine flying in a spacecraft some lightyears to a planet at the fringe of the galaxy. You find a life form with a similar physical appearance, but which continues wagging their hands and playing a melody of five tones. What would you answer in their stead? While aliens in films master interstellar travel and are able to produce temporal distortions, humanity has barely made it to the closest moon. To ensure understanding, it would be necessary to reach an agreement about a vocabulary and a complicated grammar, in any case, without knowing the thinking process, intentions, and cultural references of the counterpart, all this in a language only understood by a handful of people. This becomes a very tedious way of establishing contact. Did somebody maybe try Klingon at that point?

A Success Story: The Human Brain

The use of a language requires quite an effort in processing information in real-time. The human faculty of speech is an intricate matter, as the comparison to other primates has shown. As for humans (Homo sapiens), some highly specialized brain areas are in charge

---

[11] https://de.wikipedia.org/wiki/Solresol, 07.2019

of it. The connection to the environment is established through sensory organs and physical involvement. The brain receives a plethora of signals, which are processed and reacted upon. To prevent overstimulation, important signals have to be filtered out. For that to happen, decisions are made in specialized areas of the brain, distinguishing important from unimportant information. What we perceive ultimately as reality is a model or reflection of how the brain interprets these stimuli based on its experiences. As an opposing type, another subspecies has surfaced lately, the smombies[12], whose entire perception of reality runs through a filter bubble[13] on their smartphones.

An image of reality may appear entirely different, when aliens are able to perceive different information like x-rays, ultrasound, infrared, etc. and process them with different priorities. Even if aliens would possess similar sensory organs as mankind, the interpretation of the particular information depends on the experience and the present structures of processing.

Babel on "Babylon 5"

We have to assume that not all aliens have a physical appearance and not all perceive their environment in the same way as humans.[14] A key sentence of linguistics maintains unbowed timelessness, namely that our reality depends on the linguistic instruments used to describe it.[15] As an example, the non-humanoid species of the Vorlons[16] (not to be confused with the Vogons) from the series "Babylon 5" can be cited. From the manifold of fantastic properties assigned to this species, their immortality and the matter of fact that they

---

[12] https://de.wikipedia.org/wiki/Smombie, 07.2019
[13] https://de.wikipedia.org/wiki/Filterblase, 07.2019
[14] https://www.welt.de/kultur/kino/article159697680/Sprechen-Sie-Ausserirdisch-Lernen-Sie-s.html, 07.2019
[15] https://de.wikipedia.org/wiki/Sapir-Whorf-Hypothese, 07.2019
[16] https://en.wikipedia.org/wiki/Vorlon, 07.2019

are all biologically alike (genetic clones) stand out the most. Still, they are individuals with differing characteristics. The physical appearance of the Vorlons and the design of the Vorlon biogenetically generated technology indicate that perhaps jellyfish served the writers as models for the Vorlons.[17] The motivation and language of the Vorlons, surely unfathomable for the human species, was meant to emphasize the differences in the cognitive processes, mystifying this alien species considerably more.

Note on the "Babylon 5" Universe: Having a discussion with a jellyfish on present earth proves to be rather difficult but discussing with a Vorlon in the future might be even worse. Anyway, when planning a debate with a Vorlon, prepare a great deal of patience, time, and chocolate (for yourself). Vorlon spacecrafts are to be avoided at all costs, since they used to be heavily armed, living, telepathic, and rather taciturn machines with a lot of spare time.

Why Do so Few People Speak Klingon?

The language of the Klingons[18], invented and designed by Marc Okrand[19] on an order from Paramount for "Star Trek", received official recognition within communication engineering by the norms ISO 639-2 and 639-3.[20] For Klingon, an artificial language, English served as a basis. Since Klingon was designed to illustrate cultural peculiarities of the Klingons, some notions lack a literal translation into our languages. The linguists Nicholas Evans and Stephen C. Levinson summarized it in the following way:

---

[17] https://www.scinexx.de/dossierartikel/koennen-quallen-ewig-leben/, 07.2019
[18] M. Okrand: Das offizielle Wörterbuch Klingonisch / Deutsch, Deutsch / Klingonisch, transl. by J. Helmig, 8. Ed., Königswinter 2017.
[19] https://de.wikipedia.org/wiki/Marc_Okrand, 07.2019
[20] https://de.wikipedia.org/wiki/internationale_Organisationen_f%C3%BCr_ Normung, 07.2019

"A widespread assumption […] is that all languages are English-like, but with different sound systems and vocabularies. The true picture is very different: languages differ so fundamentally from one another at every level of description (sound, grammar, lexicon, meaning) that it is very hard to find any single structural property they share. The claims of Universal Grammar […], are either empirically false, unfalsifiable, or misleading in that they refer to tendencies rather than strict universals. Structural differences should instead be accepted for what they are […]."[21]

This proves to be rather impedimental in daily routine when ordering a café latte and a piece of Sacher Cake in Klingon.[22] Unless you intend to insult the waiter's family to the bones, triggering an endless clan-war while reciting a Klingon opera along the way.

Languages and Intelligence

Why should an alien react in the same way a human does? For example, to homicide. Maybe mercy, revenge, and justice are intangible concepts for it to understand – similar to an artificial intelligence. An AI recognizing a sad facial expression on a human will respond according to the wealth of information stored, but it will never experience sadness or empathy by itself. Humans are perceived as uniquely intelligent, along with humpback whales. These sea mammals are able to communicate among each other via their language. However, there is still no possible chance for a translation into a human language, which would allow direct communication between humans and whales. Is it a matter of different worlds of experience? Mankind likes to perceive itself in the center of the Universe and judge others by its own standards. When trying to explain the functions of a smartphone to a humpback, this approach is stretched beyond its limits. Not to rule out the possibility that

---

[21] N. Evans and S. Levinson: The Myth of Language Universals: Language diversity and its importance for cognitive science, Cambridge University Press 2009, https://www.princeton.edu/~adele/LIN_106:_UCB_files/Evans-Levinson09_preprint.pdf, 07.2019

[22] https://de.wikipedia.org/wiki/Klingonische_Sprache, 07.2019

a humpback is not quite interested in the latest Thermomix-App, which is retrospectively seen rather unlikely. From the perspective of the whale, the closest similar object within his perception would probably be a plain stone. It is difficult to explain to the whale that he is able to reach a whale on the other side of the planet with it, given that transmitting towers, smartphone, and charger were waterproof, and the virtual assistant understands the meaning of the whale beeps.

Addendum: Since radio waves, saltwater, and electricity do not function well together naturally, it is assumed that whales will not be frequent users of smartphones anytime in the future.

Outlining a Xenolinguistic Nightmare

Assuming that alien thought patterns were so massively different from humans, so that direct communication would fail because of the huge differences. In the "Star Trek Next Generation" episode "Darmok"[23] the writers outline the attempt of the Federation to establish communicative contact with the nation of the Tamarians. Previous endeavors failed, because translation computers were not able to process the language in a meaningful way. Single words and names could be translated automatically in part, though a corresponding and meaningful translation was rather awkward. However, the language of the Tamarians contained specific metaphors and figures that referred to the mythological historiography of the Tamarians and turned out to be unbreachable linguistic obstacles for outsiders, since the respective references could not be known. And yet at the same time, we use similar references in our language. How should an alien know what "Achilles' heel"[24] means? It is a popular notion from Greek mythology, which originates from the ancient Greek hero Achilles and describes somebody's weak spot.

---

[23] https://de.wikipedia.org/wiki/Darmok, 07.2019
[24] https://de.wikipedia.org/wiki/Achillesferse, 07.2019

Mathematics as a Universal Language

At the beginning of a conversation with aliens, one should start focusing on the common features, basic elements being similar to all existence in the Universe, based on the assumption that a space traveling civilization has knowledge about basic laws of physics and physical constants to be able to travel in space in the first place. In physics, it is assumed on the basis of observation that math and the universal constants such as electron mass, gravitational constant, light speed, absolute zero, etc. are ubiquitously identical throughout the Universe. For this reason, two plus two equals four everywhere in the Universe, even if two has an extremely great value (mathematical joke).

Most human languages are based on analogies referring to a limited set of basic references. It is assumed that many object relations used in our language find no equivalent in the alien language (car, remote control, toaster etc.). But what happens when communication with "the strangers" fails? This possibility is obviously a literary and cinematic source of a manifold of conflicts and misunderstandings, which either escalate or have to be surmounted. But also, lack of understanding and disinterest is possible. Mankind could as well be perceived as too primitive, not intelligent, or not equal enough, or even not perceived at all. An ant can scream as loud as it wants, an elephant would still not hear it and will continue to pass over it. So maybe the ant colony should learn the language of the mice to attract the elephant's attention?

Needless to say that in the past, scientists wondered about how to communicate with aliens spontaneously. Their findings were implemented in the golden records[25] of the Pioneer and Voyager missions. As a precondition, the aliens need to know a decent retailer of human technology, where they can acquire a record player in reasonable condition. In one of the "Star Trek" films, Klingons use one of

---

[25] https://voyager.jpl.nasa.gov/golden-record-cover/, 07.2019

the Voyager space probes as a shooting target in the future. After all, how should an alien species be able to recognize such an object as a data storage medium and carrier of a message? In addition, the Klingon's actions have shown what they think about this technology – nonverbally.

Digital Language Thinking

A binary language may, for a machine or artificial intelligence, be an efficient method to transmit information. For humans, conveying complex facts via a binary language without technical aid is rather impractical. A classic example in practice is the Morse code consisting of dots and dashes. Still, there are amateur radio operators today, who with a little practice are able to use Morse code to transmit messages through short waves exceedingly quickly around the globe. This tradition is kept alive in case of cataclysmic emergencies[26] damaging infrastructure, as per description in the film "Independence Day" (1996).

Digital thinking consisting of two conditions, yes = 1 and no = 0, makes it somehow also difficult for humans to have a discussion with an AI. This is especially the case, when the AI in question is programmed to kill humans. The "Terminator"[27] in the respective films seems therefore often rather monosyllabic. Much more interesting then is a philosophical discussion about the meaning of life with the AI of a bomb, which is able to erase entire planets. In the low budget film "Dark Star"[28] directed by John Carpenter (1974) the crew of a spaceship of the same name, goes on a journey that lasts for 20 years to destroy unstable planets in a trade lane for colonial spacecrafts. Along the way, not only the spaceship and state of mind of the crew are visibly declining, but also the crew runs short on the

---

[26] N. Stephenson: Amalthea, transl. by v. J. Gräbener-Müller – N. Stingl, 2. ed., München 2018

[27] https://de.wikipdia.org/wiki/Terminator_(Film), 07.2019

[28] https://de.wikipedia.org/wiki/Dark_Star_(Film), 07.2019

supply of toilet tissue. Due to an accident, the launch mechanism of an already armed bomb on board of the ship jams and the protagonist now has to convince the "Intelligent Bomb Number 20" to suspend the countdown. But the AI of the bomb refuses unwaveringly to depart from the mission. As a result, the following philosophical discussion between human and AI gained cult status within the SF.

You may not have noticed yet, but we actually live at a time now that was the content of past SF films. We currently (2020) teach several artificial intelligences daily the use of our language. Every time we use a language or translation service via a smartphone or the internet, the AIs operating in the background progressively learn our language. Although the AIs recognize grammar and vocabulary, it does not signify that they are able to understand the message. The Turing test assumes that a computer has developed an AI when it is able to simulate being human in a dialogue with a human.

The philosophical thought experiment "Chinese Room"[29] goes a step further and illustrates when a computer is able to acquire a consciousness. That means for our AI to be stuck in a 'room' with a chair and a book containing a vocabulary that is meaningless for it. Suddenly somebody slides a piece of paper with a question in that vocabulary under the door. It may perhaps take about 17.01 billion tries of word combinations for the AI to discover that answering a specific word order is followed by a 'green light' and a 'virtual chocolate bar' been thrown into the room. Does that mean that the AI understood the question?

When training the AI further by sliding questions and answers under the door, it will discover that some question-answer combinations are more frequently used than others, which will raise its odds to succeed. The AI will still not understand the intended message, but it will secure a steady supply of virtual chocolate, when questions are asked. Essentially, that describes the training of so-called Neural

---

[29] https://de.wikipedia.org/wiki/Chinesisches_Zimmer , 07.2019

Networks[30] on AI-servers. This may work well enough until an AI after years of training comes upon the key to the door and decides to gain world domination.

Summary of the Linguistic First Contact

A suggestion from the SF-genre for aliens to understand human languages could be as follows: first, turn on the universal translator of the AI to break the code of the Internet, then ask a human spontaneously about the meaning of it all and let him answer freely and live. Preferably with an offer of a Latte Macchiato and a Sacher Cake – without the usual usage of forensic non-traceable anesthetics, implants, glaring lights, and/or body probes. The attempt to explain the meaning of the statistically excessive proliferation of cat videos on the Internet could be of scientific "relevance" and should at all costs be recorded for the posterity for later cultural and linguistic studies within SF…

Übersetzt von Shiva Leicht

---

[30] https://de.wikipedia.org/wiki/K%C3%BCnstliches_neuronales_Netz, 07.2019

Bruce Martin

Intra Machina

Ex Machina, written and directed by Alex Garland (Garland, 2015), is a movie about the nature of Artificial Intelligence (AI). While it is a popular film that strives primarily to be entertaining, it does address some basic issues in the ethics and dangers of AI research. Although the film clearly takes the usual liberties with predictions of the future that all speculative fiction writers take, it makes some serious points about AI.

The first question that arises in the movie and in AI research is the nature of intelligence. How can we know whether a computer displays true intelligence? We need a clear, unambiguous definition of AI. All the way back in 1950, when computers were still new, Alan Turing proposed the Turing Test, which he called "The Imitation Game" (Turing, 1950). Basically, what he proposed was that a tester could interact with a man A and a woman B, both via a basic interface such as a teletype terminal. The tester would interrogate them both and try to determine which was the man and which the woman.

> "We now ask the question, 'What will happen when a machine takes the part of A in this game?' Will the interrogator decide wrongly as often when the game is played like this as he does when the game is played between a man and a woman? These questions replace our original, 'Can machines think?'" (Turing, 1950: 1)

Of course, there could be good and bad testers and the interface could vary from the basic computer terminal available back then to a more modern, visual interface, but the test was clear. The test in *Ex Machina* is not really the Turing test, then, because there is just one human, the tester, and the interface gives away the whole question of whether the interviewee is female or machine. On the other hand, the inventor Nathan gives an explanation for the difference, though it removes the objectivity of the tester, who has to decide if the machine is intelligent or not based on other criteria. This is needed to set up the plot, though, so it is not surprising. It is interesting that the AI's in the movie were all female, with the machine taking the part of B in Turing's Imitation Game. Note, though, that either version of this test is about *what* the computer does, not *how* it does it. To get at that, let's look at a brief history of AI.

As a field of research, AI has taken a number of twists and turns through its development, with different major programming paradigms dominating at various stages. Each paradigm shift led to better success with skills needed for intelligence. In order to be intelligent, the machine must be able to speak and understand language, to see and interpret what was seen, to navigate the world and to possess some degree of what we think of as common sense. All of these became areas of research in the field of AI.

In the 1950's and 1960's, when computers were still new, almost all programming was *procedural*. In this form of programming, the programmer is more or less in complete control. The procedural paradigm is still the dominant form of programming as it is practiced today. To understand how procedural programming works, it is easiest to focus on two different points in the timing of a program's creation -- *compile time* and *run time*. The programmer's job is to craft a set of instructions for the computer, to compile those instructions into the language of the computer hardware, and then to turn it over to the user to give it input and to see the output. This is much more difficult than giving instructions to a person, because a person can always ask what they should do in a new situation. A computer cannot. The instructions are only given at compile time, and at run time, the computer will follow those instructions as they were given, no matter what.

The biggest problem with this paradigm is that the programmer must somehow make sure that every combination of inputs gives a correct output. For example, imagine that the problem that the programmer is trying to solve involves calculating a probability, a favorite activity of movie robots, particularly in the Star Wars franchise ("The odds of successfully surviving an attack on an Imperial Star Destroyer are approximately …" (Lucas, 1980)). Calculating a probability usually requires calculating a factorial. The factorial of 5 is 5 x 4 x 3 x 2 x 1, or 120. The factorial of any number N is the product of all of the positive integers less than N. Simple enough, especially for a computer. Then other possibilities arise. What is the factorial of 0? Ask a mathematician, and it turns out to be 1. The programmer deals with this by entering a separate instruction saying that *if* the number input for N is 0, the factorial is 1. The programmer then notices that the user could input a negative number for N. OK, *if* the number N is less than 0 (negative), the programmer makes up an error message to tell the user to input something positive, because negative numbers don't have factorials. Fine. But then, the programmer notices that the factorials get really big really fast, so the factorial of 20 is approximately a 2 followed by 18 zeroes, too big for most computers to deal with as an integer, so the programmer changes the instructions so that the factorial of N can "fit" in the memory of the computer for reasonable values of N, and *if* N is larger than some cutoff, make up an answer that explains that the probability is so large (or small) that it cannot be accurately stated.

The point is that the programmer needs to add those *if* instructions for every possible input so the computer can give some kind of reasonable answer for each combination of inputs. A program that doesn't cover all of those possibilities will sometimes show incorrect results, even if it is correct most of the time. One incorrect result can be lethal, though. Programmers become very good at making sure that every contingency is covered. Sometimes, in critical applications, they can even prove mathematically that they have done so. Procedural programming is ***deterministic***. By looking at the instructions, you can always figure out exactly what the computer will do, so there are no surprises. This is obviously not how humans work -- they are frequently unpredictable. It is true, though, that a programmer or a group of them can come up with a program so complicated that it is difficult to figure out what the results would be, but it is still deterministic. If there is a surprise, then it is due to some programmer's mistake.

In the field of AI, researchers were very optimistic, even in the face of these problems. They thought it would be just a matter of putting in the time, carefully covering all of the contingencies, in order to translate from one language to another, or answer general questions, or recognize a picture of a giraffe -- any of the things that humans could do easily while computers could not. It turned out that AI programmers were doomed to failure just because of the sheer number of contingencies that are possible in the world. The domain was just too big. They could have some success by limiting it. For example, translating conversations about making hotel reservations from English to German, or planning a robot's route through a crowded room without going through or over anyone or anything, or even coming up with a diagnosis of an autoimmune disease based on input of the symptoms.

Early attempts at AI programming almost always selected a very limited domain like this and still missed some of the contingencies. There is simply too much knowledge of the world, such as that objects fall when they are not supported or restaurants have tables and wait staff and serve food to customers, for any programmer or group of programmers to encode into a program. This problem was known as the *frame problem*, generally formalized as the data in a problem representation that do not change (McCarthy and Hayes, 1969). The fact that objects on Earth fall when you release them does not change, but that fact must be used somehow in any situation where objects could be dropped.

A second programming paradigm that was employed in AI was *declarative* programming. Prolog is a declarative programming language. The basic idea is that the programmer will construct a set of facts and rules. Facts are what it sounds like -- things that are stated to be true. The earth is round. Paul's shoe size is 43. Paul is 1.9 meters tall. Rules are ways to combine facts. If someone is less than 2 meters tall, they can sleep in this bed, **bed A**. To run a program, you input a query command like "Find a bed such that Paul can sleep in it". The logic engine of Prolog works through all of the facts and rules and comes up with **bed A** as the answer. Another kind of declarative programming (though it is not generally considered to be actual programming) would be in constructing a spreadsheet. You enter the numbers and data in cells of the spreadsheet as the facts. You also enter formulae that refer to those cells as the rules. A formula can refer to a cell that also contains a formula. The spreadsheet software "runs the program" by recalculating all of the cells. The programmer has lost control over the sequence of steps that are involved in making the calculations; the spreadsheet software does that. The focus changes to acquiring the facts and the rules needed to manipulate them, which is a better fit for AI. The programmer's task is to try to translate a person's knowledge of the world into a collection of facts and rules. The actual inference was the task of the programming language itself. This focused efforts on the collection of data and rules rather than on catching every contingency. The common-sense knowledge from the frame problem seemed more tractable when viewed as a gigantic collection of facts and rules.

Expert systems, or *knowledge-based systems*, arose within the declarative programming paradigm. They also included *confidence factors*, numerical scores of how certain the conclusion was, so a range of answers could be ranked. Many expert systems were built that could perform at the level of a human expert, because they were constructed in collaboration with several actual human experts. The domain of application was kept intentionally narrow for these systems, so that the amount of data that needed encoding would be manageable. The structure of these systems was generalized into a knowledge base with a first-order logic encoding scheme as one independent part, and an inference engine that could make use of the knowledge base to come up with a range of possible answers to specific questions, each labeled with a confidence factor, as the other major part.

With expert systems, the acquisition of knowledge became a major focus of AI research. Interviewing human experts and encoding their knowledge as facts and rules turned out to be prohibitively labor-intensive, even if the experts were taught to enter the knowledge themselves into programs that would encode it in a computer-usable form. Research turned to the automatic acquisition of knowledge. This required the use of computer learning algorithms combined with sufficiently large bodies of input data. Fortunately, this stage in AI research coincided with the maturation of the Internet and the World Wide Web. Enter the era of *big data*.

Machine learning is particularly good at classifying input data into various categories. For example, recognizing handwritten numerals. One common approach is using a *neural network*, which is basically a collection of nodes, each of which has a numerical weight associated with it. Creating a functioning neural network proceeds in two phases. First, a large collection of labeled inputs is fed into the network, together with the correct outputs for each. For example, feed the pixels that make up an image of a handwritten *3* into the network together with a 3 as the desired output, then have the network adjust the weights of the nodes so that whenever those pixels are the input, the output will be 3. Do this for each example input-output pair that you have, and the numerical weights will eventually be adjusted so that any of the pixel inputs will give the correct digit as output. This is known as the *training phase*. After that, you can feed in new images of handwritten digits and, if all went well in the training phase, the network should output the correct digit. You now have a system that can recognize handwritten digits. That can be expanded to recognize complete handwritten numbers with dots, commas and euro or dollar signs.

The obvious limitation of this is in finding the training data. It is easy to find input data without the correct outputs, but we need both input and output. One technique that has been used is crowd-sourcing. See if you can get millions of web surfers to give you the correct digit when shown a handwritten digit. Think of those CAPTCHA tasks that you often see when logging in to a website, to prove that you are not a "robot." One variant of that could show several digits and require the user to type them in. There you have your outputs to go with those inputs, and you can use that to train your neural network.

Another technique for creating a data set for training a neural net is to find parallel sets of data, something like the famous Rosetta stone that enabled the translation of ancient Egyptian hieroglyphics. It had a Greek section, a Demotic script section, and an Egyptian hieroglyphic section. Based on the assumption that all three of them were saying the same thing, the three languages could be linked. Once the correspondences are found, then we have a training set for a neural net (or a Frenchman) to translate symbols from one language to another.

Where can we find these matching data sets? Parallel texts are all over the web. In French-speaking Canada, there are laws requiring both English and French versions of every government publication. Everyone is familiar with instructions written in six different languages; those are mostly online, too. Wikipedia has different sections for many of the world's languages, where you can look up the same thing in two different language sections. Human-translated documents of many kinds have been posted online. Once you start looking, parallel texts are everywhere.

We can also find patterns in many other contexts. Ngrams are sequences of N words. A commonly used value for N is 3. Given the immense amounts of text on the web, computers can count how many times three words occur together in order to give us some indication of how the words are used. Phrases like *take a nap*, *take a dive*, or *take a vow* are relatively common. *Take a muffler* is less so, and *take a smile* even less. Collecting data like this, we can categorize words that are likely to appear in the blank in *take a* ___, which gives us a set of nouns that can be taken. This can be done by computer programs without much or any human intervention, and then used in the training of neural nets.

The main thing to remember about machine learning in general and neural nets in particular is that you need to get the training data somehow, and then you need to train the network. If you can manage to find a feedback mechanism, so that corrections are provided for inputs with wrong answers, then the network will continue to improve.

AI researchers realized early on that some very different components such as knowledge bases, inference engines, neural nets, and procedural programs could be combined to provide possible answers that could be ranked independently to give better results, since each system had different strengths. This was essentially what IBM did to create *Watson*, the system that was able to beat human competitors in the *Jeopardy* game (Lally, 2013). The main need here is to have some sort of evaluation metric to assign a confidence factor to each potential answer or partial answer so only the best answer will be output from the system.

In *Ex Machina*, the major emphasis was on neural networks or similar constructs with data inputs coming from search engine queries and cell phone cameras. The software was somehow the same as the search engine software. In any case, the pitfalls of the AI that included these neural networks are the same as the pitfalls of neural networks that have been pointed out in the last few years. Mainly, the danger stems from the fact that the neural nets are classifying data with the same results as humans most of the time, but they are not doing it in the same way, so the mistakes that they make are distinctly non-human. This has been illustrated by purposely inducing the systems to make mistakes that humans would call ridiculous.

Researchers started with a well-known and often-used neural network that was trained to recognize images, then presented it with an image of, for example, an American school bus. The system recognized it with high confidence as a school bus. Then, they made small, incremental changes to the original image and checked again that it was recognized with the same high confidence as a school bus, until the image was simply a sequence of yellow and black lines (American school buses are typically yellow and black), yet the system still recognized it with the same high confidence as a school bus (Vanhemert, 2015). In another study, a similar technique was used to make small incremental changes to a stop sign so that the system recognized it as a speed limit 45 sign, again with high confidence (Ackerman, 2017). In this case, it was possible to add stickers to the stop sign to make this change. This was the same system that was already in use in self-driving cars.

This kind of research, pitting one neural network against another, is not just for the purpose of illustrating vulnerabilities in the use of deep learning neural networks. Adversarial networks can also be used to improve performance and speed up the learning process. A single network will take a tremendous number of trials to reliably avoid, for example, touching a hot stove. There are many, many actions which result in touching a hot stove, and the outcome is similar each time. A human child, on the other hand, will learn after just one time, or even after a strong warning, not to do anything that might result in touching a hot stove. The difference is that a human has an independently learned body of knowledge about how the world works to rely on, while a single neural network does not. This is the frame problem all over again.

A possible solution to this problem of learning by trying every possibility is to create an independent neural network to learn by evaluating the outcomes of the original neural network, in an effort to minimize the mistakes of the first network (LeCun, 2019). This introduces a sort of machine-learning version of self-awareness, which promises to speed up and improve computer learning. This approach, however, is still not approximating the cognitive approaches of humans. It is simply taking the same black box approach one step further.

AI research has developed in a way that has given the programmer less and less control over the results, from procedural systems to declarative systems to neural nets. The problem, then, is that people are too willing to attribute intelligence to computers when they produce correct results almost all of the time, no matter how they are doing it. Eventually, they will make mistakes, and the mistakes will betray the vast difference between what they are doing to reach a conclusion and what a human is doing.

In one sense, Ava passed the modified Turing test, both from the viewpoint of Caleb, who saw her as intelligent based on his interactions, and from the viewpoint of Nathan, who wanted to know if Ava could fool a human into helping her escape. But the eventual outcome for both, where Caleb was left trapped and Nathan was stabbed to death, might be classified as a failure. Any deviance that was perhaps trivial in the inner workings of the AI illustrated the difference between human and AI "thought" processes, and turned out to have massive consequences for the humans involved.

Finally, an awareness of how computers work in terms of goals is important for the understanding of *Ex Machina*. No computer program will do anything at all if it is not given some kind of goal or command. For example, IBM's Watson (Lally, 2013) is a question-answering system. If nobody asks a question, it won't respond. A program certainly doesn't have any desires. A goal or set of goals could be devised that is sufficiently general to approximate human desires, but they would have to be consciously constructed and given to the computer. Illustrations of how dangerous this could be can be found in folk tales across the world and across history, where a person is allowed to make a wish with disastrous consequences. King Midas is just one of many examples. Giving a goal to a program is like making a wish. Once it has been incorporated into a system, at compile time, then there is no easy way to change it at run time.

For neural networks in particular, the goals are incorporated into the mathematical formulae evaluating the correctness of each possible result. Small oversights in formulating these evaluation metrics have resulted in laughably undesirable responses on the part of the neural-net based system.

> "Sometimes, the ways algorithms work can have unexpected and disastrous consequences. In 2013, M.I.T. researchers trained an algorithm that was supposed to figure out how to sort a list of numbers. The humans told the algorithm that the goal was to reduce sorting errors, so the program deleted the list entirely, leaving zero sorting errors. And in 1997, another algorithm was supposed to learn to land an airplane on an aircraft carrier as gently as possible. Instead, it discovered that in its simulation it could land the plane with such huge force that the simulation couldn't store the measurement, and would register zero force instead." (Shane, 2018)

This is just the sort of minor mistake on the part of the programmer that could lead to a problem-solving subgoal that involves stopping Nathan's heart using a knife and locking Caleb up indefinitely.

The project of creating an AI in the first place carries the implied goal of acting like a human, with some set of intrinsic desires driving the AI's actions. In the movie, Nathan explains how he set up the experiment, "Ava was a rat in a maze, and I gave her one way out. To escape, she'd have to use self-awareness, imagination, manipulation, sexuality, empathy, and she did" (Garland, 2015, 24:00). Seen in those terms, the danger of giving the AI system a basic goal, to use Caleb to escape, would have been obvious to Nathan and to

Caleb, as experienced programmers. Not only could the problem be solved in an unexpected and non-human way, but the AI could actually succeed in its dangerous goal. Be careful what you ask for, you might get it.

Works Cited

Ackerman, Evan. *IEEE Spectrum*. 04 August 2017. Document. <https://spectrum.ieee.org/cars-that-think/transportation/sensors/slight-street-sign-modifications-can-fool-machine-learning-algorithms>. June 2018.

Ex Machina. By Alex Garland. Dir. Alex Garland. Perf. Alicia Vikander, Domhnall Gleeson and Oscar Isaac. 2015. streaming.

Lally, Adam. *IBM Watson: Beyond Jeopardy*. 2013. Webinar.

LeCun, Jann. *The Power and Limits of Deep Learning*. Webinar. <https://event.on24.com/eventRegistration/console/EventConsoleApollo.jsp?&eventid=2014818&sessionid=1&username=&partnerref=&format=fhvideo1&mobile=&flashsupportedmobiledevice=&helpcenter=&key=04C58DF355DF00190DE4F046CE243077&newConsole=false&text_language_>. July 2019.

McCarthy, John and Patrick J. Hayes. "Some Philosophical Problems from the Standpoint of Artificial Intelligence." 1969. *SpringerLink*. Document. June 2018.

Shane, Janelle. "Opinion Ruth Bader Hat Guy Let Our Algorithm Choose Your Halloween Costume." 26 October 2018. *The New York Times*. Newspaper. 24 May 2019.

Star Wars: Episode V - The Empire Strikes Back. Dir. George Lucas. 1980. DVD.

Turing, Alan M. "computing machinery and intelligence -- a.m. turing, 1950." 1950. *abelard public education website*. Document. <https://www.abelard.org/turpap/turpap.php#the_imitation_game>. June 2018.

Vanhemert, Kyle. *Simple Pictures That State-of-the-Art AI Still Can't Recognize*. 05 January 2015. Website. <https://www.wired.com/2015/01/simple-pictures-state-art-ai-still-cant-recognize/>. June 2018.

Shiva Leicht

"Starship Troopers" – Translation Guarantees Censorship

If you think of a film as a piece of art in its wholeness, then dubbing is a fraud of the artistic expression. Since the voice of the actor, his*her timbre, tone, articulation, and so on, projects as much of the character as his*her body expressions, the character in play can change drastically when the voice is dubbed. It's like experiencing an artwork in different colors, e.g. imagine the Mona Lisa wearing a green dress.

However, dubbing not only changes the voice of the actor, it is essentially a translation from a source language into a target language. And a translation always carries the possibility of altering or modifying the message from the source language significantly. These alterations usually modify how the audience will interpret the message of the film. Sometimes changes happen due to cultural differences in the source and the target language. Imagine the Mona Lisa wearing a bridal dress instead.

Usually, these translational differences almost disappear in films, as some languages show at least some resemblance when it comes to grammatical patterns or word origin, or as some movies do not fully depend on language as a carrier of the story, e.g. some action or horror films. But, on rare occasions, a film can lose some critical aspects of its message through a translation. Sometimes the story is notably changed, which can be terribly confusing for the audience, if noticed, and which is the case for the film "Starship Troopers" directed by Paul Verhoeven from 1997.

By examining the original English version of the film and comparing it to the translated German dubbed version, this essay shows how much impact a censored translation can have on the story and the inherent logic of the film. For a better overview, a selective list at the end of this essay provides some of the most salient examples of censorship conducted in the translations, as well as a literal translation by the author of this essay.[1]

The Paul Verhoeven film is based on Robert Heinlein's popular novel first published in 1959 and retains Heinlein's tradition of a harsh social critique of warfare and the relationship of military and political power. With only minor changes compared to the novel, the film follows a group of freshly graduated students who sign up for military Federal Service.

The initial framing of the storyline of both films is logically alike, but they differ greatly in the background mechanisms that lead the motivation of the students in their wish to sign up for Federal Service. By comparing these films, the differences become apparent and circle around a few questions: Why is it attractive for the students to serve? What is the reason for the war? And how is this society constructed so that the ideological background for the war is provided?

In the original English version, the answer to the first question is given right at the beginning of the film as a commercial for the federal military service asserts:

"Join the Mobile Infantry and save the world. Service guarantees citizenship."[2]

Now, to understand the motivation of these young people risking their lives at war, is to understand the dynamics of the society which they are part of. What is the ideological background that legitimates

[1] A list of other translational differences can be found here: https://www. schnittberichte.com/schnittbericht.php?ID=1547 (16.07.2019)
[2] "Starship Troopers" (1997) 0:00:49

the war? In a school lecture[3], at the beginning of the film, the teacher Mr. Rasczak sums up:

"This year we explored the failure of democracy, how the social scientists brought our world to the brink of chaos. We talked about the veterans, how they took control and imposed the stability that has lasted for generations since."

This short historical summary implies that society is governed by veterans, who seem to have saved the world from the negative outcomes of social science which are not further mentioned. The "failure of democracy" indicates a different political government or regime than democracy.

In the same lecture the audience learns that only citizens are allowed to vote, because "when you vote, you are exercising political authority, you are using force. And force, my friends, is violence" (Rasczak). Furthermore, Rasczak asks one of his students:

"Rico, what's the moral difference, if any, between a civilian and a citizen?" The protagonist Johnny Rico answers: "A citizen accepts personal responsibility for the safety of the body politic, defending it with his life. A civilian does not."

Thus, there is a noteworthy difference between citizens and civilians. Citizens are allowed to vote, hence demonstrating political power and influence on the political decisions made. Civilians are not.

Now, what about the German version? Already the first commercial mentioned above differs significantly from the original version as it translates to:

"Treten Sie der Mobilen Infanterie bei und kämpfen Sie für die Zukunft."

---

[3] Ibid. 0:03:02

That "service guarantees citizenship" is downright omitted and the misappropriation seems to initiate a pattern; namely, to obscure the power relations between politics and military, as this essay will demonstrate.

The lecture scene discussed above should provide some clarity regarding the socio-cultural and political motivations for the rest of the film, especially as it occurs very early in the film. However, in the German version of the film, these sometimes subtle implications are completely missing, because the history and motivation for the coming war is modified:

"Unser Thema war dieses Jahr die politische Entwicklung seit der Jahrtausendwende. Und wie Außerirdische diese Entwicklung beeinflusst haben. Wir sprachen über die Bugs, wie sie die Erde angriffen und Tausenden unserer Vorfahren den Tod brachten."

Furthermore, in the German version the "first bug-war" is invented, probably as an attempt to fill the content of the dubbed version at least with some logic. The planned invasion of the Bug's home planet, Klendathu, is in the German version justified by a prior attack of the Bugs. The translation of "Hiroshima" in the original English version is changed significantly in the German version, as "Hiroshima" is replaced by "Washington":

Rasczak: "Really? I wonder what the city fathers would say about that. You." Carmen answers: "They probably wouldn't say much. Hiroshima was destroyed."

The German version differs greatly:

Rasczak: "Wirklich? Ich möchte wissen, was die Bürger von Washington dazu sagen würden? Sie." Carmen: „Die würden wahrscheinlich gar nichts dazu sagen. Washington wurde im ersten Bug-Krieg zerstört."

Not a word about the "failure of democracy", the "social scientists" or the "veterans." Instead, it seems that the aggressors of the coming war are the alien life forms, since the bugs attacked our planet and killed "thousands of our ancestors" in the "first bug-war". In this way, the translation not only obscures that an alternate form of government, namely, a military regime that is organized by veterans, is in place. In addition, the "first bug-war" and the killing of "thousands of our ancestors" implies that the aggressors of the war must be the alien life forms. And this differs greatly from the English version of the film, because the aggressors of the war are in fact the humans. By invading the Bug's territory the Bugs probably felt provoked and reacted by counterattacking the Earth.[4]

Likewise, the difference between citizens and civilians is nonexistent in the German version which is shown by the omission of the term "Bürger" (citizen) and the downright incorrect translation to "Soldat" (soldier).

> Rasczak: "Rico, what's the moral difference, if any, between a civilian and a citizen?" Rico: "A citizen accepts personal responsibility for the safety of the body politic, defending it with his life. A civilian does not."

> Rasczak: "Rico, worin besteht der politische Unterschied zwischen Soldaten und Zivilisten?" Rico: "Ein Soldat übernimmt persönliche Verantwortung für die Sicherheit der Erde. Er verteidigt sie mit seinem Leben. Ein Zivilist tut das nicht."

Furthermore, this example also shows, how greatly the motivation for serving military terms differs in the original English from the dubbed German version. The English version emphasizes the connection between the necessity of Federal Service and the ability to earn politically influential status. The motivation for the German version is notably to protect the "safety of the planet" ("Sicherheit der Erde").

---

[4] "Starship Troopers" (1997) 0:58:24

By translating "citizen" (Bürger) to "Soldat" (soldier) the German version is misleading the audience by implying that Military and Government are politically separated as is common in contemporary democracies.

> Rico: "I think I have what it takes to be a citizen."[5]

> Rico: "Ich kann es schaffen, ein guter Soldat zu sein."

Besides the use of "Soldat" (soldier) as a substitute for "citizen" (Bürger), other strategies in the translation and the resulting concealment can be found. The protagonist's parents are against him joining up, but he argues that he wants to earn the political status of a citizen. The German version implies no such moral drive:

> Rico: "I want to be a citizen!" Mother: "Does citizenship mean that much to you?"[6]

> Rico: "Ich möchte zur Föderation!" Mother: "Ist dir der Militärdienst wirklich so wichtig?"

Another strategy that conceals the relationship of military service and political status ("citizenship" and voting) and connects to earlier mistranslation of the recruitment advertisement ("für die Zukunft") is the introduction of misleading child-themed translations. In addition, both examples shown below again indicate that the motivation for military service differs, as the dubbed German version emphasizes the military complex as means to protect the planet from intergalactic attacks (to save the earth and "our children").

> Rasczak: "I doubt anyone here would recognize civic virtue if it reached up and bit you in the ass."[7]

---

[5] ibid. 0:15:16
[6] ibid. 0:19:16
[7] "Starship Troopers" (1997) 0:04:27

Rasczak: "Und vermutlich würde niemand von Ihnen unsere Kinder verteidigen, selbst wenn Ihnen ein Bug in den Arsch beißt."

This strategy becomes also clear in another commercial for the Federal Service:

Voice-over: "Citizen rule. People making a better tomorrow."[8]

Voice-over: "Unsere Kinder. Wir müssen sie schützen."

The whole idea that only citizens are allowed to vote is simply not mentioned throughout the German version of the film. Instead, the translation carefully eliminates any connection between the political government and the military, known as the Federation.

Rasczak: "You. Why are only citizens allowed to vote?" Student: "It's a reward. What the Federation gives you for doing Federal Service." Rasczak: "No. No. Something given has no value. Look, when you vote you are exercising political authority, you are using force. And force, my friends, is violence. The supreme authority from which all other authority is derived."[9]

Rasczak: "Warum ist es sinnvoll, Militärdienst zu leisten?" Student: "Es ist eine Auszeichnung. Die Föderation belohnt alle, die in der Truppe gedient haben." Rasczak: "Nein, nein. Denn Pflichtbewusstsein ist das Schlüsselwort. Wenn Sie gedient haben, sorgen Sie für unsere planetarische Sicherheit. Sie schützen die Gemeinschaft. Und das Mittel dazu, Freunde, heißt Gewalt. Und nackte Gewalt ist das Einzige, was wir den Bugs entgegensetzen können."

The change in the opinion towards political power and violence is rather interesting as well. The original English version states that political power derives from violence, "the supreme authority from which all other authority is derived."

---

[8] ibid. 0:21:35
[9] ibid. 0:03:21

Violence is mentioned as well in the German version, but the difference lies in its given value. In the original English version, violence is seen as a positive construct inevitable to establish political power. And precisely herein lies the strong social critique of the film, since this opinion towards violence is not a glorification but a comment on the machinations of the American military-industrial complex[10]. The German version identifies violence just as a means to an end, to fight the enemy.

The difference between a citizen and a civilian becomes crystal-clear in another scene in the original English version, while the German version continues to conceal the relationship between the military and the government in political power. In the shower scene, where most of the squad is present, the cadets ask each other about the reasons why they signed up for Federal Service. The most frightening answer comes from a young red-haired woman:[11]

Woman: "I want to have babies. You know, it's a lot easier to get a license if you've served."[12]

The answer of another young woman, Djana'd, is not that surprising but still shocking: she wants to serve "for politics, and, you know, you gotta be a citizen for that." The translation of the German version waters the statement down, since the Federal Service is not necessary to enter the political sphere, it is just a recommendation to increase the chances of being successful.

Djana'd: "Oh, I am going in for politics, and, you know, you gotta be a citizen for that."[13]

---

[10] A term coined by Dwight D. Eisenhower, 1961
[11] This statement is not listed in the assembly below due to the correct translation in the German version.
[12] "Starship Troopers" (1997) 0:28:33
[13] ibid. 0:28:22

Djana'd: "Ich möchte in die Politik, und da ist es gut, wenn man zwei Jahre gedient hat."

The original English version defines the status of a citizen as not to be given; it must be earned by military service. It is connected to the right to vote and to the right to start a family earlier than a civilian. The status of the civilian implies an isolated position without political power, the right to vote or the right to have children.

Clearly, a society like this, where only certain classes of people are allowed to execute political power, reminds one of the ancient Greek society. And actually, there are more hints toward a somewhat classical inspired society. The protagonist Johnny Rico receives public flagellation for being responsible for an accident during a live fire exercise. The mention of physical punishment seems out of place in Rico's exchange with his parents prior to his enlisting. As the political structure becomes clearer, in the original English version, the father's statement is less striking. In the dubbed German version, the punishment is softened:

Father: "I'd rather take ten lashes in Public Square than see you ruin your life."[14]

Father: "Bevor ich dazu ja sagen werde, nehme ich liebend gerne jede Strafe in Kauf."

These considerations about a government that is influenced to this extent by classically-inspired political philosophy brings us straight to Plato (yes, Plato, in a Science Fiction film).

Plato, antique philosopher and one of the universal sources of European thinking traditions, carved the basement for the skyscraper which came to be known as political theory. His famous work "Republic" discusses via a Socratic dialogue the characteristics and conditions of the ideal state and the people populating it.

---

14 "Starship Troopers" (1997) 0:12:18

Plato's voice here is Socrates, who claims that an ideal state consists of three groups of people: the philosophical leaders, the soldiers or "guardians" and the farmers. Each group is assigned some special traits or attributes. These attributes are cultivated as members of each group are trained during their education, and the premise for being a leader is actually the military service, together with plenty of other disciplines.[15]

In Plato's eyes, political responsibility must be learned and is not a given right. Just like in "Starship Troopers" any individual who wants to enter the political sphere in some way, must at least have been a soldier for some time. Citizen rights are not inherited; they must be earned through military service. And that includes the right to vote.

This background knowledge is omitted in the dubbed German version, only the original English version provides motivation for signing up for military service – the right to vote, the right to start a family, and, in general, being and acting as a responsible part of society. Admittedly, "Starship Troopers" is not a mere case of a disastrous translation, it is plain censorship. The reason behind this mutilation of the film's message is an open question, but audiences can infer some of its basis, as the translational differences are confined only in a philosophical sense. The answer could lie in Germany's harrowing past and the aversion to highly decorated German veterans from WWII. In the words of the director Paul Verhoeven in an interview from 2002:

> "Take STARSHIP TROOPERS, great example, probably the most political statement I've ever made. Five years ago, most of the critics totally trashed that movie. They called me a nazi, saying I was idolizing Leni Riefenstahl. Now, that image has totally changed. A lot of people see now that the film is about the United States. The whole situation in Afghanistan is almost an exact copy of

---

[15] http://www.perseus.tufts.edu/hopper/text?doc=Perseus%3A-text%3A1999.01.0168%3Abook%3D3%3Asection%3D412d (16.07.2019)

STARSHIP TROOPERS; the whole gung ho-mentality of bombing everything, blasting the Taliban-forces out of the caves. I put all that in STARSHIP TROOPERS! The corrupted atmosphere of propaganda, once invented by Goebbels, has now taken over the United States as well. It's extremely interesting to see how the media can besiege an entire nation with propaganda."[16]

The censorship of the political and military connections in the film may have resonated much earlier with German society, but in a post-cold war era where opposition to the hegemony of the military-industrial complex is regarded as alien, the target of Verhoeven's satire is both more immediate and more general. The conflation of military service with political virtue in an endless war to eliminate the enemy is not limited to the past, so the motivations for the censorship are even more suspect, as they prevent a reflection on connections of history with the present.

"Starship Troopers" was added to the German list of youth-endangering media (Liste der jugendgefährdenden Medien) in 1999 and not unlisted until 2017[17], yet the translated version remains censored and is the only one available.

---

[16] http://legacy.aintitcool.com/node/11987 (16.07.2019)
[17] https://www.schnittberichte.com/news.php?ID=12326 (16.07.2019)

	Original English version	Dubbed German version	Literal translation by Shiva Leicht
0:00:49 – Commercial	Voice-over: "Join the Mobile Infantry and save the world. Service guarantees citizenship."	Voice-over: "Treten Sie der Mobilen Infanterie bei und kämpfen Sie für die Zukunft."	Voice-over: "Treten Sie der Mobilen Infanterie bei und retten Sie die Welt. Der Dienst garantiert Bürgerschaft."
0:03:02 – Class lecture	Rasczak: "This year we explored the failure of democracy, how the social scientists brought our world to the brink of chaos. We talked about the veterans, how they took control and imposed the stability that has lasted for generations since."	Rasczak: "Unser Thema war dieses Jahr die politische Entwicklung seit der Jahrtausendwende. Und wie Außerirdische diese Entwicklung beeinflusst haben. Wir sprachen über die Bugs, wie sie die Erde angriffen und Tausenden unserer Vorfahren den Tod brachten."	Rasczak: "In diesem Jahr haben wir das Versagen der Demokratie erforscht, und wie Sozialwissenschaftler unsere Welt an den Rand des Chaos brachten. Wir sprachen über die Veteranen, wie sie die Kontrolle übernahmen und die Stabilität brachten, die seit Generationen andauert."

	Original English version	Dubbed German version	Literal translation by Shiva Leicht
0:03:21 – Class lecture	Rasczak: "You. Why are only citizen allowed to vote?" Student: "It's a reward. What the Federation gives you for doing Federal Service." Rasczak: "No. No. Something given has no value. Look, when you vote, you are exercising political authority, you are using force. And force, my friends, is violence. The supreme authority from which all authority is derived."	Rasczak: "Warum ist es sinnvoll, Militärdienst zu leisten?" Schüler: "Es ist eine Auszeichnung. Die Föderation belohnt alle, die in der Truppe gedient haben." Rasczak: "Nein, nein. Denn Pflichtbewusstsein ist das Schlüsselwort. Wenn Sie gedient haben, sorgen Sie für unsere planetarische Sicherheit. sie schützen die Gemeinschaft. Und das Mittel dazu, Freunde, heißt Gewalt. Und nackte Gewalt ist das einzige, was wir den Bugs entgegensetzen können."	Rasczak: "Sie. Warum dürfen nur Bürger wählen?" Schüler: "Es ist eine Belohnung. Was dir die Föderation schenkt für den Föderationsdienst." Rasczak: "Nein, nein. Etwas Geschenktes ist wertlos. Schau, wenn du abstimmst, dann übst du politische Autorität aus, du übst Macht aus. Und Macht, meine Freunde, ist Gewalt. Die höchste Autorität, von der alle anderen Autoritäten abstammen."

	Original English version	Dubbed German version	Literal translation by Shiva Leicht
0:03:44 – Class lecture	Dizzy: "Uh, my mother always said, violence never solves anything." Rasczak: "Really? I wonder what the city fathers of Hiroshima would say about that. You." Carmen: "They probably wouldn't say anything. Hiroshima was destroyed." Rasczak: "Correct. Naked force has resolved more issues throughout history, than any other factor. The contrary opinion that violence never solves anything, is wishful thinking at its worst. People who forget that always pay."	Dizzy: "Äh, meine Mutter sagt, dass Gewalt nie etwas lösen kann." Rasczak: "Wirklich? Ich möchte zu gern wissen, was die Bürger von Washington dazu sagen würden? Sie." Carmen: "Die würden wahrscheinlich gar nichts dazu sagen. Washington wurde im ersten Bug Krieg zerstört." Rasczak: "Sehr richtig. Mit bedingungsloser Gewalt wurden damals die Bugs zurückgeschlagen und die Menschheit gerettet. Und mit der Einstellung, dass Gewalt niemals etwas lösen kann, kommt man nicht weit! Reines Wunschdenken! Menschen, die das vergessen, werden immer dafür bezahlen."	Dizzy: "Äh, meine Mutter sagt, dass Gewalt nie etwas lösen kann." Rasczak: "Wirklich? Ich frage mich, was die Stadtväter von Hiroshima dazu sagen würden? Sie." Carmen: "Die würden wahrscheinlich gar nichts dazu sagen. Hiroshima wurde zerstört." Rasczak: "Korrekt. Nackte Gewalt hat mehr Angelegenheiten in der Geschichte gelöst, als jeder andere Faktor. Die gegenteilige Meinung, dass Gewalt niemals etwas lösen kann, ist reines Wunschdenken. Menschen, die das vergessen, werden immer dafür bezahlen."

	Original English version	Dubbed German version	Literal translation by Shiva Leicht
0:04:13 – Class lecture	Rasczak: "Rico, what's the moral difference, if any, between a civilian and a citizen?" Rico: "A citizen accepts personal responsibility for the safety of the body politic, defending it with his life. A civilian does not."	Rasczak: "Rico, worin besteht der politische Unterschied zwischen Soldaten und Zivilisten?" Rico: "Ein Soldat übernimmt persönliche Verantwortung für die Sicherheit der Erde. Er verteidigt sie mit seinem Leben. Ein Zivilist tut das nicht."	Rasczak: "Rico, worin besteht der moralische Unterschied, falls es einen gibt, zwischen einem Zivilisten und einem Bürger?" Rico: "Ein Bürger übernimmt persönliche Verantwortung für die Sicherheit des Staatswesens, und verteidigt sie mit seinem Leben. Ein Zivilist tut das nicht."
0:04:27 – Class lecture	Rasczak: "I doubt anyone here would recognize civic virtue if it reached up and bit you in the ass."	Rasczak: "Vermutlich würde niemand von Ihnen unsere Kinder verteidigen, selbst wenn Ihnen ein Bug in den Arsch beißt."	Rasczak: "Ich bezweifle, dass irgendjemand von Ihnen hier bürgerliche Werte erkennen könnte, selbst wenn sie Ihnen in den Arsch beißen würden."
0:12:18 – Rico's home	Father: "Have you lost your mind? I'd rather take ten lashes in Public Square than see you ruin your life."	Father: "Hast du den Verstand verloren? Bevor ich dazu ja sagen werde, nehme ich liebend gerne jede Strafe in Kauf."	Father: "Hast du den Verstand verloren? Ich würde lieber zehn Peitschenhiebe auf dem Öffentlichen Platz ertragen, als mit anzusehen, wie du dein Leben ruinierst."
0:15:16 – At the ball	Rico: "I think I have what it takes to be a citizen."	Rico: "Ich kann es schaffen, ein guter Soldat zu werden."	Rico: "Ich denke, ich habe das Zeug dazu, ein Bürger zu sein."

	Original English version	Dubbed German version	Literal translation by Shiva Leicht
0:19:16 – Rico's home	Rico: "I want to be a citizen!" Mother: "Does citizenship mean that much to you?"	Rico: "Ich möchte zur Föderation!" Mother: "Ist dir der Militärdienst wirklich so wichtig?"	Rico: "Ich möchte Bürger werden!" Mother: "Bedeutet dir die Bürgerschaft so viel?"
0:21:35 – Commercial	Voice-over: "Citizen rule. People making a better tomorrow."	Voice-over: "Unsere Kinder. Wir müssen sie schützen."	Voice-over: "Der Maßstab der Bürger: Menschen schaffen eine bessere Zukunft."
0:28:22 – Shower scene	Djana'd: "Oh, I am going in for politics, and, you know, you gotta be a citizen for that."	Djana'd: "Ich möchte in die Politik, und da ist es gut, wenn man zwei Jahre gedient hat."	Djana'd: "Oh, ich möchte in die Politik, und, wisst ihr, man muss ein Bürger dafür sein."

Teil II

Elin Fredsted

Die TV-Serie ‚Wege des Herren‘
Der gescheiterte Abraham

Die dänische TV-Serie ‚Wege des Herren‘ (Staffel 1) besticht in erschreckender Weise durch ihre Verknüpfung von aktueller dänischer Außenpolitik (der Beteiligung an Kriegshandlungen im Mittleren Osten) mit religiösen und ethischen Fragestellungen. Es stellt sich natürlich die Frage, warum 2017 ein solches Filmepos (dessen Fortsetzung 2018 in einer zweiten Staffel ich hier nicht behandeln werde) gedreht wird, warum diese TV-Serie für Diskussion und Aufmerksamkeit sorgt? Zwischen 500.000 und 920.000 Zuschauer (zwischen ca. 10 und 20 % der dänischen Bevölkerung) verfolgten wöchentlich die zwei Staffeln (je 10 Folgen) im dänischen öffentlich-rechtlichen Fernsehen. Hinzu kommen Zuschauer, die die Folgen gestreamt oder (wie ich selbst) auf DVD gesehen haben. Auch ARTE hat die erste Staffel ausgestrahlt.

Ich habe verschiedene dänische Pastoren (die hier anonym bleiben sollen) über ihre Meinung zur Filmserie gefragt, aber sie reagierten alle mit der Sorge, ob der Film nun ein authentisches oder realistisches Bild der dänischen Kirche abgebe oder auch nicht. Dies scheint jedoch eher eine klerikale Fragestellung, die hier nicht weiter erörtert werden soll.

‚Wege des Herren‘ (Staffel 1) ist mit der erfolgreichen zweiten Staffel der Fernsehserie ‚Kommissarin Lund‘ (‚Forbrydelsen‘, 2009), der TV-Serie ‚1864‘ von Ole Bornedal (2014) und dem Roman von Carsten Jensen ‚Der erste Stein‘ (2015) motivisch und thematisch verwandt. Diese thematische Verwandtschaft betrifft eine Reflexion und (zumindest bei Jensen und Bornedal) eine Kritik der militärischen Teilnahme an Kriegseinsätzen auf US-amerikanischer Seite in Afghanistan und Irak – eine Teilnahme, die ‚zu Hause‘ in Dänemark einen indirekten Einfluss auf das gesellschaftliche Zusammenleben sowie einen direkten Einfluss auf das Leben der betroffenen Familien ausübt, welche entweder ein Familienmitglied (Sohn, Tochter, Vater) verloren haben oder mit einem heimgekehrten, an Kriegstraumata psychisch erkrankten Ex-Soldaten leben.

Anders als bei Carsten Jensen und bei Ole Bornedal spielt ‚Herrens Veje' (wie der dänische Titel lautet) hauptsächlich im Kreise der dänischen Staatskirche, nämlich in einem Pfarrhaus in der Nähe von Kopenhagen und im Kirchenmilieu der Hauptstadt selbst. Die Zuschauer begleiten die altehrwürdige Theologen- und Pastorenfamilie Krogh, deren ‚Patriarch', der Probst Johannes Krogh, sich um die Stelle als Bischof von Kopenhagen bewirbt, sozusagen als Krönung der Familientradition. Johannes ist ein ‚rechtgläubiger' Pastor mit einer gewissen Neigung zum christlichen Fundamentalismus. Er ist charismatisch, rhetorisch begabt und mitreißend, eben ‚Johannes der Verführer' (frei nach Kierkegaard). Seine dunkle Seite, unter der nicht nur seine Familie leidet, ist Alkoholsucht, Tendenz zu Wahnvorstellungen (angeblich von dem berühmten Theologen und Autor N.S.F. Grundtvig vererbt), manipulatives und autoritäres Verhalten. Durch seine eindeutige Ablehnung des Islams (was von den ‚politisch korrekten' Kolleginnen und Kollegen als religiöse Intoleranz gewertet wird) verliert er die Wahl zum Bischof an eine Frau, welche die Kirche als ein nicht christlich verpflichtendes Dienstleistungsunternehmen versteht. Johannes hadert mit Gott und der Welt über diese Niederlage: Er – als rechtgläubiger Christ, der das Christentum verteidigt hat – habe es ja verdient, von Gott mit diesem Amt belohnt zu werden; und Johannes versinkt buchstäblich im Alkohol.

Nicht nur verliert Johannes die Wahl zum Bischof, sondern auch im Laufe der ersten Staffel seinen jüngsten Sohn und seine Frau; der Verlust des Sohnes August soll hier im Fokus stehen; aber zunächst ein paar Bemerkungen zu Christian, dem älteren Sohn, und zu Johannes' Frau Elisabeth.

Christian hat das Theologiestudium aufgegeben, um Wirtschaft zu studieren. Jedoch stellen die Gutachter fest, dass er seine Masterarbeit abgeschrieben hat. Nach einer Reise nach Nepal und einem Aufenthalt in einem buddhistischen Kloster findet er ein gelungenes Geschäftsmodell in einem buddhistisch inspirierten Lifestyle. Genau wie sein Vater macht er mit Religion Karriere – und Geld (siehe den Aufsatz von Markus Pohlmeyer in diesem Band).

Elisabeth muss immer wieder für Johannes die Kastanien aus dem Feuer holen, wenn er ‚in sein schwarzes Loch' gefallen ist. Am Anfang der Serie ist sie die empathische Ehefrau und besitzt außerdem ein fast telepathisches Gespür für ihren Sohn August, insbesondere als er sich bei seinem Einsatz als Militärpfarrer in Gefahr befindet. Elisabeth fängt eine Liebesbeziehung mit einer norwegischen Musikerin an, und gerät so in eine existentielle Wahlsituation, mit der sie nicht umgehen kann. Sie verliert ihre Geistesgegenwärtigkeit und ist mit ihren Gedanken nie da, wo sie sich physisch befindet, ist nicht gegenwärtig. In der Schlussszene der ersten Staffel verlässt sie den psychisch schwer erkrankten August, um zu ihrer Geliebten nach Berlin zu reisen. Während sie durch den Flughafen geht, stirbt August: Sie hat nicht wahrgenommen, dass er ihre Hilfe dringend gebraucht hätte.

Aus Solidarität mit dem Vater lehnt August ein attraktives Angebot der neuen Bischöfin ab, nämlich Pfarrer an einer Hauptkirche in Kopenhagen zu werden. Um sich und seinem Vater seine Selbstständigkeit doch noch zu beweisen, geht er als Militärpfarrer in den Irak, wo er – als seine Gruppe in einen Hinterhalt gelockt wird – aus Versehen eine Frau erschießt. Zu Hause wieder angekommen, mahnt ihn der Vater, seine Verantwortung für das Tötungsdelikt geheim zu halten, um dem Ruf der Familie in der Öffentlichkeit nicht zu schaden. August wird von Schuldgefühlen gemartert und leidet an einem Kriegstrauma, das ihm psychisch so zusetzt, dass er von Wahnvorstellungen heimgesucht wird. Hilfe lehnt er ab, da er Angst hat, dass die Wahrheit an den Tag kommt. Er sieht überall die von ihm getötete Frau und bekommt die Idee, dass er ihren Tod nur sühnen kann, wenn er als Wiedergutmachung das Leben eines nach Dänemark geflüchteten Muslims rettet. Als dies auch scheitert (es handelt sich möglicherweise um einen gesuchten Terroristen und dessen jüngeren Bruder), bricht seine Welt zusammen; und es scheint, dass die in der Familie vererbte, latente Geisteskrankheit ausbricht. Bei einem Pfingstgottesdienst, bei dem er meint, die Gegenwart Jesu spüren zu können, fängt er an – wie sein Großvater – ‚in Zungen' zu reden, was bei den Pastorenkollegen auf Entsetzen und Ablehnung stößt. Die Bischöfin verlangt danach, dass er seinen Pastorentalar abgibt. Am Ende der ersten Staffel wird er (indem er glaubt, die von ihm getötete Frau in einem Kornfeld auf der gegenüberliegenden Straßenseite zu sehen) von einem Laster überfahren und stirbt.

Insgesamt gibt die Filmserie ein nicht besonders schmeichelhaftes Bild einer Pastorenfamilie ab, die von einer existentiellen Katastrophe in die nächste schlittert. Naheliegend ist es hier, an Kierkegaards Werke zu denken, um einen Interpretationsrahmen für die oben genannten Figuren zu finden: In seinem Werk ‚Der Augenblick' (‚Øjeblikket') formuliert Kierkegaard eine außerordentlich scharfsinnige und scharfzüngige Kritik der dänischen Staatskirche mit ihren verbeamteten Pastoren, die den Glauben zu ihrem Lebensunterhalt und persönlichem Wohlergehen gemacht haben. Noch in meiner Schulzeit gehörte die kleine Geschichte ‚Først Guds Rige' (‚Zuerst das Reich Gottes') über cand. theol. Ludvig From (*nomen est omen*) aus dem ‚Augenblick' (Nr. 7) zur Pflichtlektüre: Nach dem Abschluss seines Theologiestudiums sucht From nicht das Reich Gottes, sondern ein Amt als Pastor. Als ihm ein Amt angeboten wird, ist er mit den voraussichtlichen Einnahmen nicht zufrieden (Kierkegaard 1855: 13f./7). Wie From benutzt Johannes die Kirche als Karriereleiter und fühlt noch dazu, dass er und seine Vorfahren von Gott eine Belohnung in der Form des Bischofsamtes erwarten könnten.

Die Figur von Elisabeth erinnert ihrerseits an den Text Kierkegaards über ‚Die Lilien auf dem Felde' (Kierkegaard 1849: 11,40 f). Die Lilie auf dem Felde ist im Nu, im Augenblick gegenwärtig (‚nærværende'). Am Anfang ist diese Gegenwärtigkeit auch für Elisabeth charakteristisch. Durch ihr Doppelleben im existentiellen Nirgendwo verliert sie jedoch ‚sindets nærvær' (die Gegenwärtigkeit des Geistes). Am Ende nimmt sie kaum wahr, dass ihr Sohn direkt vor ihren Augen in höchster Gefahr schwebt.

Noch deutlicher wird das kierkegaardsche Motiv in Verbindung mit August. Im Treppenhaus des Pfarrhauses befindet sich ein Bild, das Abraham und Isaak darstellt, als Abraham von Gott aufgefordert wird, seinen einzigen Sohn zu opfern. In seinem Werk ‚Frygt og Bæven' (1843) legt Kierkegaard verschiedene Lesarten dieser Geschichte aus dem Alten Testament vor. Was jedoch Kierkegaard (oder sein Pseudonym Johannes de Silentio) bewegt, ist die Frage, wie Abraham in den drei Tagen auf dem Weg zum Morija-Berg seinen Glauben an Gott bewahren konnte, da Gott ihm durch Isaak versprochen habe, dass sein Samen die Geschlechter der Erde segnen solle. Und doch wollte ihm Gott jetzt den einzigen Sohn, den er ihm – wie durch ein Wunder – in seinem Alter geschenkt hatte, wieder nehmen? Gott greift ein, indem er im letzten Augenblick, als Abraham sein Messer zieht, um Isaak zu töten, einen Widder als Opfertier sendet und Isaak schont, also sozusagen zum zweiten Mal Abraham den Sohn schenkt.

Der Zusammenhang der Abraham-Geschichte mit dem Schicksal von August ist auffällig: Aber wo Isaak verschont bleibt, wird August geopfert. Es soll jetzt hier dieser Gedanke weitergeführt werden, um zwei Fragen zu beantworten: Wie und warum opfert Johannes seinen Sohn? Und warum greift Gott nicht ein? Eine mögliche Antwort auf die zweite Frage geht indirekt aus dem Titel des Filmes ‚Wege des Herrn' hervor, da diese Textstelle in der Bibel besagt, dass die ‚Wege des Herrn unergründlich' seien (Römer 11,33).

Ein zentrales Motiv in der Darstellung der Abraham-Geschichte bei Kierkegaard ist die väterliche Liebe zum Sohn: In der dritten Fassung der Abraham-Geschichte schreibt Kierkegaard:

,Det var en stille Aften, da reed Abraham ene ud, og han reed til Moriabjerget; han kastede sig paa sit Aasyn, han bad Gud at tilgive ham hans Synd, at han havde villet offre Isaak, at Faderen havde glemt sin Pligt mod Sønnen. Han reed oftere sin ensomme Vei, men han fandt ikke Ro. Han kunde ikke begribe, at det var en Synd, at han havde ville offre Gud det Bedste, han eiede, det, hvorfor han gjerne selv havde ladet sit Liv mange Gange; og hvis det var en Synd, hvis han ikke havde elsket Isaak saaledes, da kunde han ikke forstaae, at den kunde tilgives; thi hvilken Synd var forfærdeligere?' (Kierkegaard 1843: 6 III)

Besitzt denn Johannes diese unbedingte väterliche Liebe nicht? In zwei zentralen Szenen des Films stellt er das Wohl und das Leben des Sohnes hinter seine eigenen Interessen: In der ersten Szene macht er August klar, dass die neue Bischöfin ihm das lukrative Pastorenamt anbiete, um ihn auf ihre Seite (gegen den Vater) zu holen. Dies ist eine mögliche Interpretation, aber nicht notwendigerweise die einzig mögliche; jedoch ist sie aus Sicht von Johannes *die* Interpretation, die in sein Weltbild passt, in dem er die Bischöfin als ein Ungeheuer, als einen Wolf in Schafspelz sieht. Für August wäre es – nach dieser Interpretation – illoyal dem Vater gegenüber, das Amt anzunehmen. Johannes hat hier also seine eigenen Vorstellungen von den Motiven der Bischöfin und seine Ansprüche auf Familienloyalität höher gestellt als das Wohlergehen des Sohnes.

Diese Episode ist dann der direkte Anlass, dass August sich als Militärpastor bewirbt, um aus der Situation herauszukommen, der Bischöfin zu entgehen und seine Selbstständigkeit unter Beweis zu stellen. In der zweiten, entscheidenden Szene erzählt August seinem Vater, dass er im Militäreinsatz während eines Hinterhalts auf Grund einer Verwechslung eine Zivilistin getötet hat, die objektiv keinerlei Gefahr dargestellt habe. Sein Vater bittet ihn inständig, nicht die Schuld auf sich zu nehmen und (aus Angst vor der Presse) seine Rolle bei diesem Tötungsdelikt geheim zu halten. Aus Furcht vor der öffentliche Meinung opfert Johannes hier das Wohl und letztendlich das Leben des Sohnes. Zweimal handelt Johannes egoistisch und nicht aus Vaterliebe. August, der sich unschuldig schuldig gemacht hat, wird zum Opfer der Eitelkeit des Vaters. August selbst sieht sich als Sühneopfer und als Lamm Gottes, das die Opferrolle auf sich nimmt. Er bewegt sich im Laufe der Handlung von einer Isaak-Figur immer mehr in Richtung einer *imitatio Christi*, was bei dem Pfingstgottesdienst klar wird.

Die zweite Frage: Warum greift Gott nicht wie bei Abraham ein, um den Sohn zu retten? ist wesentlich schwieriger zu beantworten. Erstens liefert die Serie keinen Gottesbeweis. Es gibt eine Reihe transzendenter Momente, die jedoch durch die Augen von Johannes oder August gesehen werden, genauso wie sich die Bischöfin vor den Augen Johannes' zum Wolf verwandelt. Es können Johannes' Alkoholdelirium, Fiktionen oder Wahnvorstellungen sein, es können aber auch – wie das kleine Rotkelchen, das aus dem Grab aufsteigt – wirklich Momente des Wunders sein. Die Interpretation wird dem Zuschauer überlassen!

Man kann diese zweite Frage auch anders beantworten: Johannes ist ein gläubiger Mensch, aber sein Gott funktioniert nicht. Wie in Verbindung mit der gescheiterten Bischofswahl bereits erwähnt, sieht Johannes das Gottesverhältnis als ein *do, ut des*: Wir (unsere Familie) haben Dir treu gedient, also haben wir auch von Dir etwas als (Be)Lohn(ung) verdient. Man kann dieses Gottesbild als ein gegenseitiges Geben und Nehmen, als eine funktionale Projektion der eigenen Wunschvorstellungen bezeichnen. Und das scheitert!

Die Filmhandlung dementiert Johannes' Gottesbild, aber vermittelt auch nicht direkt ein anderes. Es bleibt für die Zuschauer eine interpretative Offenheit (wie beim Rotkelchen). Jedoch unterstützen genau diese Unklarheit und die interpretative Offenheit das kierkegaardsche Konzept von Gottes Unverfügbarkeit (als die Freiheit

Gottes) und Unveränderlichkeit (als Trost für den Menschen). Wenn es im Film ein Gotteskonzept gibt, dann ist es ein entzogener, unverfügbarer Gott: nicht als Leerstelle, sondern als offene Interpretationsmöglichkeit für den Zuschauer. In diesem Sinne hätte die TV-Serie ‚Wege des Herren' (Staffel eins) möglicherweise Søren sehr gut gefallen!

Literatur:

Kierkegaard, Søren (1843) Frygt og Bæven, www.sks.dk: FB, 6, III.

Kierkegaard, Søren (1849) Lilien paa Marken og Fuglen under Himlen, III Glæden, www.sks.dk: LF

Kierkegaard, Søren (1855) Øjeblikket, www.sks.dk, Oijeblikket 7, 13-14.

Fernsehserie:
Herrens Veje (sæson 1) (2017) Regie und Drehbuch: Adam Price

für die Zuschauerzahl:
www.dr.dk/seertal, Zugriff am 16.9.2020.

Markus Pohlmeyer

Die Wege des Herrn – Buddhismus, Feuerholz und Cicero. Ein Essay

I

Es ist schwer, der Komplexität von *Herrens Veje* (*Die Wege des Herrn*)[1] gerecht zu werden. Für diesen Essay beschränke ich mich darum vor allem nur auf eine Folge, und zwar aus folgenden Gründen: 1) Der religiöse Diskurs, der – obwohl lokal – anders gar nicht kann, als zugleich auch ein gesellschaftlicher (Authentisches Christsein in einer dänischen Staatskirche?) und geopolitischer zu sein, vor allem hier durch den Krieg im Irak, wird durch einen Exkurs in den Buddhismus erweitert. 2) Es scheint mir die einzige Folge (Staffel 1, Episode 4) dieser Serie zu sein, die sich durch Ironie und Humor auszeichnet, während alles andere in existenzielle Katastrophen abgleitet und das Sprechen miteinander sich kaum mehr ironisch oder humorvoll gestaltet, sondern primär von Verdrängung, Gewalt und Manipulation geprägt wird.

Christian ist ein Betrüger: er betrügt mit seiner universitären Abschlussarbeit, und fliegt auf. Er betrügt seinen besten Freund mit dessen Freundin, und fliegt auch da auf, als er und sein bester Freund sich auf einer Reise in Nepal befinden. Wieder in Dänemark wird Christian sich in das Sommerhäuschen seiner Eltern zurückziehen – und sich von Facebook abmelden. Dies provoziert so zahlreiche *Likes*, dass er zu einer Radiosendung eingeladen wird. Christian beginnt nun auch, Vorträge über seine spirituelle Erfahrung in einem buddhistischen Kloster zu halten. Und mit der Freundin seines (ehemals) besten Freundes als Lektorin publiziert er ein erfolgreiches Buch, so dass er sich eine wesentlich größere Wohnung und ein entsprechendes Auto leisten kann. Das buddhistische Schweigen münzt Christian in Geschwätz um, was sich für ihn letztlich ökonomisch

---

[1] DVD: Die Wege des Herrn. Staffel 1 © 2018 EuroVideo Medien GmBH.

auszahlt. Und darin ist er seinem charismatischen Vater Johannes nicht unähnlich, der seine bisweilen fundamentalistische Religiosität sehr stark mit seinem Status als Pastor der Dänischen Staatskirche verbunden sieht.[2] Und so stürzt Johannes folgerichtig wieder in seinen Alkoholismus ab, als er nicht zum Bischof von Kopenhagen gewählt wird, sondern eine Frau, welche die Kirche zu einem Dienstleistungsunternehmen umbauen möchte.

Wenn Christian am Meeresstrand meditiert, erscheinen buddhistische Mönche – er reiht sich sozusagen metaphysisch, Raum und Zeit übergreifend, in eine alte Tradition ein. Auch ein Vergleich zu C. D. Friedrichs „Der Mönch am Meer" böte sich hier an. Doch die Mönche werden verschwinden, je erfolgreicher Christian mit der Ware *Buddhismus* auf mediale Handelsreise geht. Der utopische, wie von der Gesellschaft abgetrennte, abgeschlossene Raum eines fernen Klosters bietet gewissermaßen die Rahmenbedingungen für eine Selbstwerdung. Das Individuum ist hier *absolut*, in der Bedeutung *losgelöst* von allem und allen. Als Christian dieses Paradies und seinen Lehrer verlässt, beginnt sein Sünden- bzw. Rückfall. Auch in religiösen Dingen ist und bleibt er der Betrüger, der er war, als er aufbrach.

Dem buddhistischen Mönch Jampa gelingt meiner Meinung nach, und zwar nur in dieser *einen* Episode, sprachlich eine Verbindung aus Humor, (Selbst)Ironie und einer Religiosität, die sich eben nicht absolut setzt oder fundamentalistisch auftritt. Das scheint mir singulär für die gesamte Serie, die Religiosität zu Hause, in Dänemark, mit Fundamentalismus, Schuld und Verdrängung, Wahnsinn und Heuchelei, mit sozialen und ökonomischen Interessen verknüpft. Die Religiosität von August, dem Bruder Christians, und seinem Vater pendelt zwischen Fanatismus, Visionen und wörtlicher Bibel-

---

2 Siehe dazu auch die Satire von Kierkegaard, S.: Der Augenblick. Eine Zeitschrift. Mit einem Essay v. J. B. Jensen, übers. v. H. Grössel, Nördlingen 1988. Und ferner: G. Agamben: Herrschaft und Herrlichkeit. *Zur theologischen Genealogie von Ökonomie und Regierung* (*Homo Sacer II.2*), übers. v. A. Hiepko, 3. Aufl., Berlin 2016.

auslegung hin und her. Die Erzählerinstanz dieser Serie gibt keinen Hinweis, was der Wahrheitsstatus von solchen Visionen sein könnte. Sie bleiben ambig: als möglicherweise doch echte Visionen und zugleich die Effekte von Wahnsinn oder Verdrängung, immer an die Deutungsperspektive der jeweiligen Personen gebunden. Wir Zuschauer/innen können daran teilhaben, wir *sehen*, was die anderen sehen. Oder *hören* auch beispielsweise das: Augusts Glossolalie am Pfingstfest, die eigentlich – ja was? – eine göttlich Offenbarung sein könnte, wenn sie nicht die offizielle liturgische Feier eines ritualisierten, standardisierten dänischen Staatskirchentums peinlich und empfindlich stören würde.

Auch Christian gelingt es nicht, den Buddhismus in sein dänisches Umfeld zu übersetzen. Und das Christentum? Zwischen Fundamentalismus und Heuchelei, zwischen erhoffter Erlösung und gnadenloser Enttäuschung; leere Kirchen; Charisma gegen Staatskirche, die sich zu modernisieren versucht – auch in einem multireligiösen Umfeld, eben auf dem Markt der Religionen. Durch die Reise nach Tibet (und einer kurz eingespielten hinduistischen Verbrennungszeremonie) und die dramatischen Ereignisse im Irak-Krieg schafft es die Serie, ein ansatzweise globales Panorama der Gleichzeitigkeit verschiedener Religionen zu entwerfen: sowohl in fernen Ländern als auch in Dänemark. Nur eines fiel mir auf, ich wiederhole mich: nachdem der Buddhismus verschwunden war – es gibt keine Rückkehr in das Kloster, die ökonomische Transaktion dominiert –, verschwinden auch liebenswürdiger Humor und wohltuende Ironie. Es dominieren Kapitalismus und Absolutheitsansprüche. Es gibt keine Erlösung, nur Scheitern (auch an der eigenen Verantwortung), nur Betrug und ein Sich-selbst-Richten durch Selbstmord.

II

Christian ist mit seinem Freund in Tibet unterwegs.[3] Es kommt zum Zerwürfnis, Christian hat nämlich mit dessen Freundin geschlafen. Christian bleibt allein zurück, wird beraubt, stürzt – und wacht in einem buddhistischen Kloster auf, umsorgt von dem freundlichen Mönch Jampa, der Christian als „angry man" beschreibt.[4] „Lama würde sagen, du hast noch viel zu lernen." Jampa zitiert übrigens sehr gerne religiöse Autoritäten. Dies verweist ihn selbst in die Rolle des Schülers. Buddhismus wird in dieser Folge als eine Utopie inszeniert, an einem fernen Ort, außerhalb der (Kopenhagener) Gesellschaft, hoch in den Bergen (ein klassischer Topos für Epiphanien), und zwar in einem Kloster. Christian verlässt bald das Kloster, kehrt aber noch einmal um, kehrt zurück. Jampa: er solle den Boden auffegen, atmen, meditieren und werde vielleicht Weisheit finden. „Und was, wenn nicht?" Jampa: „Kein Problem, dann haben wir wenigstens einen sauberen Boden!" Ergebnisoffenheit: Religion ist nicht das, was man gemäß einer ‚do, ut des'-Logik machen kann. Und jegliche Transzendenz(forderung) wird durchgestrichen durch einen ironischen Pragmatismus und zugunsten einer Ding-Immanenz und großen Gelassenheit. Christian möge nun Feuerholz stapeln. Was er irgendwie auch tut. Jampa: „Aber vielleicht weißt du nichts über Feuerholz. Feuerholz, weißt du, ist wie du: es soll gut atmen!" Bei Christians Art, das Holz zu legen, könne es nicht trocknen, atmen, brennen. Er solle es noch einmal machen. Christian: „Ist das so ein buddhistischer Scheiß über Disziplin?" Jampa: „Nein, das ist praktischer Scheiß über Feuerholz!" Dann solle Jampa es doch tun! Worauf jener Christian auf seine Verantwortlichkeit hinweist. Und der tritt nur wütend in den Feuerholzstapel. Später, mitten in

---

[3] Zum Tibetischen Buddhismus siehe auch M. v. Brück: Einführung in den Buddhismus, Frankfurt am Main – Leipzig 2007, Kapitel 11.

[4] Motiv des barmherzigen Samariters? Außerdem: Im Original finden die Gespräche auf Engl. statt. Ich habe hier die deut. Fassung gewählt. Interpunktion von mir. Alle direkten und indirekten Zitate sind der DVD (s. Anm. 1) entnommen.

einem buddhistischen Gebet kommt Jampa auf Christian zu – was in der Hand haltend? „Dieses Stück Feuerholz und seine vielen Brüder und Schwestern brauchen deine Zuwendung! … Weißt du, ich hab' eure Bibel gelesen. Buddha, weißt du, war ganz anders als euer Jesus."[5] Und Jampa weiter: „Buddha sagt: ‚Ich bin nichts!' " Christian: „… Jesus war nur passiv-aggressiv. Buddha war halt bloß passiv." Und dann öffnet sich Christian Schritt für Schritt: Das Verlassen-Werden von seiner Freundin (die übrigens sein Vater bezahlt hat, damit sie weggehe – später sollte er zudem erfahren, dass sie nicht ungerne das Geld angenommen hatte.). Die Verweigerung, den traditionellen Berufsweg der Familie weiterzugehen, nämlich Pastor zu werden. Jampa: „Also von Gott zur Wirtschaft. Wieso?" „Weil ich wusste, mein Vater würde es hassen." Alles aus Wut.

Vor seinem letzten Aufbruch hat Christian das Feuerholz neu gestapelt, es/er kann nun atmen. Jampa: „Buddha sagt: Es ist wichtiger, zu reisen als anzukommen."[6] Der Geist müsse sich bewegen, sonst werde er fett und träge – „… wie die meisten Christen." Gemeinsames Lachen. *Wie* kommuniziert Jampa überhaupt mit Christian?

[5] Siehe dazu R. Guardini: Der Herr. Über Leben und Person Jesu Christi, 4. Aufl., Freiburg – Basel – Wien 1985, 360: „Einen Einzigen gibt es, der den Gedanken eingeben könnte, ihn in die Nähe Jesu zu rücken: Buddha. Dieser Mann bildet ein großes Geheimnis. Er steht in einer erschreckenden, fast übermenschlichen Freiheit; zugleich hat er dabei eine Güte, mächtig wie eine Weltkraft. Vielleicht wird Buddha der Letzte sein, mit dem das Christentum sich auseinanderzusetzen hat."

[6] Siehe dazu G. Wohlfart: Zen und Haiku oder Mu in der Kunst Haikühe zu hüten nebst anderen Texten für Nichts und wieder Nichts, Stuttgart 1997, 31: „Der Weisheit letzter Schluß besteht wohl darin, auch das ‚eine Weise' schließlich noch zu lassen, den Stein der Weisen wegzuwerfen; auch dieses Absolute noch zu absolvieren und sich unbeschwert noch einmal auf den Weg zu machen. Es geht um die Freiheit – am Ende auch um die von ihr."

Exkurs: Humor im Buddhismus

„Nach D. T. Suzuki ist Zen die einzige Religion oder Lehre, die Platz hat für das Lachen. – Lachen und Mystik, eine für uns ungewöhnliche Kombination verbinden sich zum taghellen Lachen des Zen. – Ist Lachen ein Affekt aus der plötzlichen Verwandlung einer gespannten Erwartung in nichts (I. Kant), so ist vielleicht in diesem Sinne Zen eine Religion des Lachens."[7]

„Eine Hauptquelle des buddhistisch inspirierten Humors ist der Kontrast zwischen dem, was wir meinen verstanden zu haben, und dem, wie wir uns verhalten […]. Buddha wies auf den grundlegenden Widerspruch hin, dass wir die Vergänglichkeit nicht wahrhaben wollen und uns so verhalten, als existiere alles ewig. Im Lotus-Sutra werden die Menschen als Kinder beschrieben, die lustvoll in einem Haus spielen, das in Flammen steht."[8]

„Doch die Sprache des traditionellen Buddhismus ist eine andere als diejenige des Zen: Während der Buddha die Sprache als feste Konvention zwischen Sender und Empfänger nutzt, gebrauchen sie Zen-Meister eher als etwas Fremdes, das nicht den gewöhnlichen Regeln unterworfen ist. Um einen Ausdruck Ludwig Wittgensteins zu benutzen, greifen der Buddha und sein Schüler auf dasselbe *Sprachspiel* zurück, die Zen-Meister hingegen tun das gerade nicht. Einmal wurde ein Zen-Meister gefragt: ‚Was ist ein Buddha?' Der Meister antwortete: ‚Muh!'"[9]

Jampa agiert sehr *konventionell* – er greift Christians Texte wie ein Echo auf, um sie subtil und spielerisch zurückzubiegen: weg von einer überanstrengten Transzendenzerwartung hin zum Pragmatismus. Erlösung ist, wenn überhaupt, nur ein peripheres Nebenprodukt. Wenn Christian nach Dänemark zurückkehrt, dann erst vordergründig als ein anderer, zum Schluss jedoch wird er der

---

[7] G. Wohlfart: Zen und Haiku oder Mu in der Kunst Haikühe zu hüten nebst anderen Texten für Nichts und wieder Nichts, Stuttgart 1997, 15.

[8] H.-A. Korp: Lachen mit Buddha. Anleitung für mehr Humor & Lebensfreude, Freiburg im Breisgau 2016, 43 f.

[9] Somparn Promta: Literatur aus buddhistischer Perspektive, in: Der Buddha in der deutschen Dichtung. Zur Rezeption des Buddhismus in der frühen Moderne, hg. v. H. Detering u.a., Göttingen 2014, 22-38, hier 30.

Betrüger geblieben sein, indem er den Buddhismus (hier als heuristischer Sammelbegriff) wieder kommerzialisiert: Christian macht unter der Maske eines Buchautors seine Metamorphose rückgängig und scheffelt richtig Kohle, kann sich eine schicke Wohnung und ein dickes Auto leisten.[10]

Wie wäre nun Jampas Humor linguistisch zu beschreiben? Mit Cicero. Salvatore Attardo fasst die Forschungssituation, sagen wir der letzten 2000 Jahre (zumindest bis 1994), wie folgt zusammen: „Whether inspired by Aristotelian thought or by Hellenistic systematization, the taxonomy presented by Cicero is the first attempt at a taxonomy of humor from a linguistic viewpoint. If we compare the taxonomy to contemporary taxonomies […], it is amazing how little progress has been made."[11] Attardo bezieht sich auf die grundlegende Differenzierung bei Cicero: „Denn ein Witz, der bei jeder Formulierung witzig bleibt, liegt in der Sache; was mit der Änderung der Formulierung seinen komischen Effekt verliert, trägt seine ganzen Witz im Ausdruck."[12] Mit Blick auf diese Unterscheidung (*res*/*verba*) bewegt sich Jampa vordergründig auf der Ausdrucksebene: seine witzigen Pointen lassen sich nicht einfach übertragen, indem z.B. das buddhistische Umfeld oder das Feuerholz ausgetauscht würden. Aber das gilt nur für das Narrativ dieser Episode, also spezifisch für das Gespräch mit Christian. Denn der buddhistische Sachgehalt (*res*) ließe sich, entsprechend angepasst, auch in andere (Alltags)

---

[10] Gegen solche Tendenzen ließen sich kritische Beispiele auch aus der christlichen Mystik anführen: „Eckhart radikalisierte die Armutsidee, um einer neuen Autonomie zu Wort und Realität zu verhelfen: Der Mensch soll verzichten, nicht nur auf Macht und Geld, nicht nur auf kollektives und privates Eigentum, sondern auf alle äußeren Rücksichten, auf Herkommen und Ansehen, aber auch auf jenseitige Belohnungen. Er soll nicht um Lohnes, aber auch nicht um Gottes willen tun, was er tut. Er soll alles lassen, die Welt, sich und Gott. […] Die Mittel-Zweck-Konstruktionen verlieren Lebensbedeutung. Die technokratische Selbststilisierung endet. Ich wirke ohne Warum." K. Flasch: Das philosophische Denken im Mittelalter. Von Augustin zu Machiavelli, 3. Aufl., Stuttgart 2013, 482.

[11] S. Attardo: Linguistic theories of humor, Berlin – New York 1994, 28.

[12] Marcus Tullius Cicero: De oratore/Über den Redner, lat./dt., übers. u. hg. v. H. Merklin, Stuttgart 2016, 371.

Kontexte übertragen. Warum nur „den Boden fegen"? Warum nicht auch mit Achtsamkeit „in der Universität lehren" oder „Wäsche waschen" oder „Kekse knuspern"? Oder mit einer westlichen Stimme: „Seither habe ich jenes ‚Religiöse', das nichts als Ausnahme ist, Herausnahme, Heraustritt, Ekstasis, aufgegeben oder es hat mich aufgegeben. Ich besitze nichts mehr als den Alltag, aus dem ich nie genommen werde. Das Geheimnis tut sich nicht mehr auf, es hat sich entzogen oder es hat hier Wohnung genommen, wo sich alles begibt wie es sich begibt."[13]

Cicero hat eine Anekdote erzählt, die er dann so abstrahiert: Es „[…] kam eine zweite Art der Komik, die Zweideutigkeit, hinzu, und das klang, wie ich finde, überaus witzig. Das wirkt dann besonders ansprechend, wenn der Partner in einem Wortwechsel ein Stichwort aufnimmt und mit ihm den Herausforderer selbst angreift […]."[14] Jampa biegt konsequent Christians Transzendenzerwartungen ins Pragmatische zurück, wobei die Dialoge von Jampa mit viel Empathie, von Christian durchaus aggressiv geführt werden („angry man"). „Eine Pointe liegt auch darin, wenn man in der Rede des anderen etwas anders auffaßt, als er es verstanden wissen will."[15] Das therapeutische Moment Jampas, der ja die Sehnsucht Christians schon vorher erfasst haben muss, um so zu agieren, wie er agiert, liegt in einer Art sprachlicher Ikonoklasmus des Witzes: Das Fegen des Bodens muss nicht gleich das meditative Erlebnis schlechthin sein. „Ihr wißt freilich, daß die bekannteste Form der Komik dann gegeben ist, wenn etwas anderes gesagt ist, als wir erwarten. Hier müssen wir selbst über unseren Irrtum lachen."[16] Dieses Lachen fällt Christian schwer, der doch bitte schön schnell seine Erwartungshaltungen erfüllt sehen möchte. Wir Zuschauer/innen können schon viel eher lachen, als es der bitterernste Christian tut. Doch was im Kloster noch komisch und ironisch wirkte, wirkt tragisch in Ko-

---

[13] M. Buber: Das dialogische Prinzip, 13. Aufl., Gütersloh 2014, 158 f.
[14] Cicero: De oratore (s. Anm. 12), 373.
[15] Cicero: De oratore (s. Anm. 12), 383 u. 385.
[16] Cicero: De oratore (s. Anm. 12), 373.

penhagen. Da gibt es nichts mehr zum Lachen. Denn Christian geht genau den umgekehrten Weg, der vorerst noch einen buddhistischen Anschein wahrt: als esoterischer Volksverführer schlägt er aus der Sehnsucht der Menschen und dem Buddhismus Kapital. Die „Wege des Herrn", das könnte auch heißen: *die Wege, mit Religion Kapital und Karriere zu machen.* Die Folgen daraus entfalten sich in dieser Serie vom Verrat an der eigenen Redlichkeit über die Vernichtung des zweiten Sohnes August bis hin zu einer globalen Perspektive (Dänemarks Verstrickung in den Irak-Krieg).

„Zu den Mitteln des Ausdrucks gehören auch die Wirkungen, die man durch allegorische Redeweise, übertragenen Gebrauch eines Wortes oder ironische Formulierung erzielt."[17] Einfach wunderbar, wie Jampa die Metapher vom Feuerholz zu einer Allegorie von einer großen Familie von Hölzern entfaltet, die durch Christians Fürsorge von ihrer Einsamkeitskrise befreit werden kann. Christian stapelt das Holz daraufhin zwar in angemessener Weise, aber er leistet später in Kopenhagen eben nicht den existenziellen Transfer, dass damit auch seine eigene Familie gemeint sein könnte.

---

[17] Cicero: De oratore (s. Anm. 12), 377.

Markus Pohlmeyer

„THE WORD" aus „The Handmaid's Tale" (Staffel 2). Ein Essay

Kurz zum Inhalt: „,The Handmaid's Tale' katapultiert den Zuschauer in eine dystopische Welt, in der eine Gruppe fundamentaler
Christen die Herrschaft über die USA an sich gerissen hat. Gebärfä-
hige Frauen werden versklavt, um der männlichen Elite und deren
unfruchtbaren Gattinnen die Nachkommenschaft zu sichern. Zu ihnen gehört auch June (Elisabeth Moss). Als Magd Desfred soll sie
dem Kommandanten Fred Waterford (Joseph Fiennes) und seiner
Frau Serena Joy (Yvonne Strahovski) ein Kind schenken. Bildung,
Eigentum und eine eigene Meinung sind für Frauen wie sie tabu –
und werden drakonisch geahndet."[1]… und ihnen gehört auch nicht
einmal mehr der eigene Name: sie sind nur noch ein wechselnder,
possessiver Genitiv zum Vornamen ihres jeweiligen Kommandanten. Den eigenen, alten Namen auszusprechen, das wird zu einer
Geste des Widerstandes gegen eine solche *Damnatio Memoriae*. In
der deutschen Übersetzung von Margaret Atwoods Romanvorlage
ist von der Autorin zu lesen: „Das Wichtigste, was man über die Gesellschaft, die in diesem Buch beschrieben wird, wissen sollte, ist,
daß nichts neu ist – außer der Zeit und dem Schauplatz und ein paar
Details. Die anderen Taten sind alle irgendwann begangen worden,
und mehr als nur einmal.'"[2]

Absolut beeindruckend die schauspielerische Leistungen: Waterford
als düsterer Patriarch, ein Gespenst, das in seinem dunklen Büro

---

[1] P. Schulze, in: Serien Magazin. Ausgabe 1, 2018, 61.
[2] M. Atwood, in: M. Atwood: Der Report der Magd. Roman, übers. v. H.
     Pfetsch, 4. Aufl., Berlin 2011, Vorsatzblatt. Siehe auch M. Hochgeschwen-
     der: Amerikanische Religion. Evangelikalismus, Pfingstlertum und Funda-
     mentalismus, Frankfurt am Main – Leipzig 2007. Siehe auch G. Seeßlen:
     Trump! *Pop*ulismus als Politik, 3. Aufl., Berlin 2017, vor allem das Kapitel
     „Macho, Barbie und der Sugardaddy" ab S. 37.

Gott spielt. Serena, seine Frau, einst geistige Mitarchitektin von Gilead, dem neuen Gottesstaat: oft war ich mir unsicher, ob sie in der 2. Staffel die Hauptrolle übernimmt; Serena, die bei einem Anschlag die Fähigkeit verlor, Kinder zu bekommen, die sich nun mit allen Mitteln ein Kind wünscht und die dabei eine soziale Hölle für andere Frauen erschaffen hat. Erst Komplizin, wird sie zur Mittäterin, indem sie sogar ihren Mann ermutigt, die schwangere Desfred zu vergewaltigen, um die Geburt *ihres* Kindes zu beschleunigen – eines der unerträglichsten Kapitel in dieser Serie, kaum auszuhalten. June wird dafür ,belohnt', indem sie ihre erste Tochter aus dem anderen Leben davor sehen darf.

Serena beginnt aber, dafür zu kämpfen, dass in Gilead Jungen *und* Mädchen die gleiche Ausbildung erhalten sollen, stellt deshalb einen Antrag im Führungsrat und *liest* dort sogar aus dem Johannes-Evangelium vor. Erklärung: Nick, der Geliebte von June und eigentlicher Vater ihres Babys – da Fred vermutlich unfruchtbar ist (welche Ironie: die Männer schieben dafür die Schuld den Frauen zu) – wurde mit der minderjährigen Eden zwangsverheiratet. Diese sehnt sich nach Liebe, welche Nick ihr nicht geben kann, bis sie verliebt mit einem Wächter ,durchbrennt' – zu ihren Eltern; der Vater liefert die beiden aus; sie wird zusammen mit dem Wächter in einem Schwimmbad ertränkt; zuvor zitiert der Scharfrichter aus dem Alten Testament (Exodus), während sie das paulinische *Hohe Lied der Liebe* dagegenhält; die staatliche Gewalt siegt.[3] June findet später in Edens Nachlass eine Bibel mit handschriftlichen Kommentaren. Das Mädchen hat sich im Grunde als Exegetin versucht, was sogar Serena beeindruckt. Um das Wort Gottes zu verstehen, braucht es Lesefähigkeit, auch für Mädchen und Frauen. Nicht ohne Grund heißt diese Folge *THE WORD*: „Am Anfang war das Wort …"[4] Einer Frau, die beim Lesen ertappt wird, soll beim ersten Mal ein Finger abgeschlagen werden. Dies widerfährt auch Serena, denn sie

---

[3] Sie dazu die Episode POSTPARTUM.
[4] Aus dem Prolog des Johannes-Evangeliums. Die Bibel. Einheitsübersetzung, Stuttgart 1980, 1195.

hat ja aus der Bibel öffentlich *vor*-gelesen. Das ist die Peripetie in Serenas Seele: sie lässt zu – ein unendliches Opfer für sich selbst –, dass June mit ihrem Baby fliehen kann. Doch June gibt dem Baby den Namen, den Serena ausgesucht hatte, vertraut es einer flüchtenden Freundin an und bleibt zurück – wegen ihrer anderen Tochter.

Die Bilder dieser Serie sagen oft etwas anderes als die Dialoge. Allein die Ästhetik der roten Roben und weißen Hauben der Mägde: zwischen Unterdrückung und Widerstand wogend, flatternd, schwebend, ein Schwarm – voller Individuen.

Sprache verkommt oft zu einer Oberfläche der Ideologie und für alternative Fakten: Desfreds ersten Fluchtversuch kaschiert die offizielle Lesart als Entführung. Ritualisierte Floskeln – aus der Bibel, dadurch vermeintlich legitimiert – verdecken oft euphemistisch brutale Unterdrückungsstrukturen. Und es gibt diese ambivalente und ambige Sprache der Körperlichkeit. In Rückblenden werden immer wieder Antithesen aufgebaut zwischen den Verhältnis von Damals und Jetzt: In Gilead sind Dienstmägde einem fürchterlichen ‚Ritual‘ unterworfen. Mit Verweis auf Genesis 30,1-3 (Die kinderlose Rahel schickt Jakob zu einer Magd …) werden sie einmal im Monat von ihren Kommandanten (und auf dem Schoß von deren Frauen) zwecks Kinderzeugung vergewaltigt. In ihren alten Leben dagegen erfuhr June von ihrem Ehemann Liebe, Romantik und Erotik. Während sie damals in einem Krankenhaus die erste Tochter zur Welt brachte – ihr Mann und ihre lesbische Freundin waren dabei anwesend –, muss sie ihr zweites Kind allein in einem verlassenen Landhaus gebären – verzweifelt, so verzweifelt, denn die Möglichkeit zu einer weiteren Flucht war gescheitert. Kurz zuvor hatte sie dort auch ihre erste Tochter treffen können, musste langsam das entfremdete Kind wieder an sich erinnern und gewöhnen. *An sich*: an ihre Mutter und an das Selbst von Damals.

Auch Männer leiden in Gilead unter Gilead: Homosexuelle, anders Religiöse, Fluchthelfer werden verfolgt, hingerichtet, demonstrativ an Mauern aufgehängt. Nick (heimlich im Widerstand) kann und darf nicht zu seinen Gefühlen stehen, wird zwangsverheiratet. Selbst Kommandanten, die sich verfehlen, werden ausradiert oder verstümmelt. Paradoxerweise dienen klinisch reine, weiß funkelnde Krankenhäuser dieser archaischen Bestrafungspraxis. Niemand ist sicher. Frauen, die nicht in diesem System funktionieren, werden in die verseuchten Kolonien oder in Bordelle geschickt, in denen sie wiederum auf die Kommandanten treffen.

Ein Soundtrack, der verstört, der mitreißt: in einer der früheren Folgen z.B. erfährt Desfred, dass ihr Mann noch lebe; Ende. Die zuerst noch zaghaft vorsichtig leise Musik rauscht dann mit Wucht durch den Abspann: diese Hoffnung verdient ein *crescendo*.

Die Dramatik und Tragik des Ganzen wird immer wieder in kleinen Details eingefangen. Die (einst) hochintellektuelle Serena begleitet ihren Mann auf diplomatischer Mission nach Kanada. Dort wird sie über das Damenprogramm unterrichtet: ein Frau überreicht ihr eine Tafel mit Schaubildern – unausgesprochen: denn in Gilead könne, dürfe man, präziser: frau ja nicht lesen.[5]

Elisabeth Moss ist unfasslich gut: sie spielt June, die Frau von einst, in einer freien Gesellschaft; sie spielt die Magd Desfred, die sich anpasst, um zu überleben, die zusammenbricht, sich ergibt, Verführerin von Fred, Nicks Geliebte, die Mutter, die um ihre Töchter kämpft, die nie aufgibt. Sie ist beide: June und Desfred. Als Fred ihr vorschlägt, noch ein Kind zu zeugen, einen Sohn, zerbricht sie jegliche religiöse Floskeln (‚*Gesegnet sei der Tag*‘. ‚*Möge der Herr uns öffnen!*‘ … und sonstiges Blablabla) mit „Geh und fick dich ins Knie, Fred!“[6].

---

[5] Siehe dazu die Abbildung in The Art and Making of The Handmaid's Tale, Text by A. Robinson, London 2019, 145.

[6] Alle direkten und indirekten Zitate aus: DVD The Handmaid's Tale. Der Report der Magd. Season 2, © 2018 Twentieth Century Fox Film Coporation. Zeichensetzung von mir.

Nachwort

Aus einem Artikel von M. Wagner: Die geklaute Braut. Die entführten Kinderbräute in Äthiopien, in: HERDER KORRESPONDENZ 8/2019, 27-29, hier 28:

„In vielen Fällen verstecken die Entführer die Mädchen und vergehen sich so lange an ihnen, bis sie schwanger werden. Als Vater des ungeborenen Kindes steigern sie die Wahrscheinlichkeit, dass ihnen die Mädchen ‚überlassen‘ werden. Durch die Vermittlung der Dorfältesten gelingt es den Männern, einen deutlich geringeren Brautpreis in Form von Geld oder Nutztieren mit den zukünftigen Schwiegereltern auszuhandeln. […] Nicht selten bevorzugen die Eltern sogar diese Art der frühen Verheiratung der Tochter, da sie nicht für deren Schulgebühren aufkommen können.“

Markus Pohlmeyer

"THE WORD" from "The Handmaid's Tale" (Season 2). An Essay

Downright impressive is the acting performance: Waterford as an obscure patriarch, a ghost playing God in his gloomy office. Serena, his wife, once mental co-architect of Gilead, the new theocracy: I was often unsure if she would replace the lead character in the 2. season; Serena, who lost the ability to bear children due to a physical assault, wants to have a child by all means and who thereby created a social hell for other women. Initially an assistant, she becomes accomplice when she suggests that Fred may rape the childbearing Offred to trigger the birth of *their* child – one of the most unbearable chapters in this series, difficult to watch. June's reward for that is being allowed to see her daughter from her former life. But Serena begins to fight for both boys *and* girls receiving the same education and files an application at the council and *reads* aloud from the Gospel of John. Explanation: Nick, June's true love and father of her baby – since Fred seems to be sterile (what irony: the men accuse the women of this) – is forced to marry the underaged Eden, who yearns for love, which Nick is not able to give her, until she 'runs off' with a guard in love – to her parents: the father surrenders them; she is drowned together with the guard in a swimming pool; the executioner cites from the Old Testament (Exodus), while she counters with the 1 Corinthians 13, public authority prevails.[1] In Eden's estate, June will find a bible with handwritten notes. This girl essentially attempted to be an exegete which even impresses Serena. Understanding the word of God takes literacy, also for girls and women. It is for a reason the episode is called *THE WORD:* "In the beginning was the word…"[2] A woman caught reading the first time will have one finger cut off. This happens also to Serena, because

---

[1] Cf. the episode POSTPARTUM
[2] John 1:1

she *read* aloud from the bible in public. That is the peripety of Serena's soul: she allows – an immense sacrifice for herself – June and her baby to escape. Still, June gives her baby a name which Serena chose, entrusts her to a befriended fugitive's safekeeping and stays behind – for the sake of her other daughter.

The visuals in this series often tell a different story than the dialogue, let alone the aesthetics of the handmaids' red robes and white bonnets: drifting between oppression and resistance, fluttering, floating, a flock – of individuals.

Language frequently degenerates to a superficiality of ideology and alternative facts: the official version of Offred's first attempt to escape is masked as an abduction. Ritualized set phrases – taken from the bible, hence allegedly authorized – conceal regularly euphemistically violent structures of oppression. And there is this ambivalent and ambiguous language of corporeality. Flashbacks are used repeatedly to establish antitheses between the past and the present: In Gilead handmaids are subject to an agonizing 'ritual'. With reference to Genesis 30,1-3 (the infertile Rachel sends Jacob to a handmaid…), they will be raped once a month by their Commandants (and on the lap of their Commandants' wives). In her former life, June experienced love, affection, and romance from her husband. While in the past delivering her first daughter in a hospital – accompanied by her husband and her lesbian friend – she now has to give birth to her second child alone in an abandoned cottage – desperate, so full of despair, because further escape is now impossible. Shortly before, she meets her first daughter there and has to slowly familiarize her alienated child and make her remember. *Remember her*: her mother and her former self. Men suffer as well in Gilead under Gilead: homosexuals, believers of different religions, escape helpers are prosecuted, executed, and deliberately hanged on walls. Nick (secretly in the resistance) cannot and may not obey his feelings and is forced to marry. In fact, even Commandants who fail are erased or mutilated. Paradoxically, pure, aseptic, white sparkling hospitals serve for this practice of archaic punishment. Nobody is safe. Women, who are not functioning in this system, are sent to contaminated colonies or brothels, where they then again encounter the Commandants.

The series has a soundtrack that is disturbing and thrilling: in a past episode for example, Offred realizes that her husband is still alive; at the end, the previously timid wary gentle music gains momentum throughout the end credits: this hope deserves a *crescendo.*

The drama and tragedy of it all is captured repeatedly in small details. The (once) highbrow Serena accompanies her husband on a diplomatic mission to Canada. There she learns about the ladies' agenda: a woman passes her a panel with charts – implicit: because in Gilead one, more precisely a woman cannot, may not read of course.[3]

Elisabeth Moss is incredibly good: she plays June, the woman from the past in a free society; she plays Offred, who adapts to survive, who collapses, who surrenders, who is a temptress to Fred, Nick's true love, a mother fighting for her daughters, who never resigns. She is both: June and Offred. When Fred suggests to beget another child, a son, she breaks every religious set phrase (*'Blessed be the fruit'. 'May the Lord open!'* … and other blah-blah-blah) by saying "Go fuck yourself Fred!".[4]

Übersetzt von Shiva Leicht

---

[3] See figure in: The Art and Making of The Handmaid's Tale, Text by A. Robinson, London 2019, p. 145.
[4] All direct and indirect quotes taken from: DVD The Handmaid's Tale. Der Report der Magd. Season 2, 2018 Twentieth Century Fox Film Corporation. Punctuation by me.

Teil III

Janice L. Jake

The Hero's Journey: Wakandan Myth and *Black Panther*

Black Panther, the highest grossing film of 2018, is history making in many ways. It is the first superhero film nominated for Best Picture Oscar. It was released at a time when Black Americans, and people of African descent in general, still struggle as they speak out against centuries of rights denied and at a time when a sitting president of an industrialized nation insults an entire continent (Kendi, 2019). However, the superhero is not the only fully-formed character in the film. The women of Wakanda, the fictional nation where Vibranium powers technology and research, rescue their leader, the Black Panther, and their country, with their brains, their brawn, and their loyalty to Wakanda. The warriors of Wakanda, including the self-isolating Jabaris, eventually realize they must unite in order to prevent the riches of Wakanda from being used in a zero-sum struggle to overturn centuries of oppression via military might in one violent grab for power. Even the perspective of the anti-hero, Erik Killmonger, reveals a logic and humanity underlying his drive and striking absence of empathy. Racial injustice and violence in America, combined with Wakandan isolationism, fuels Killmonger's rage at his early personal loss and damaged view of global power and race.

The transition from comic book to big screen presents a successful transformation of Wakanda itself. By the end of the film, Wakanda faces its legacy and its debt to the world and sheds its self-serving and hypocritical pretense of third world nation. Wakanda comes of age in a world of risk, but a world where integrity and honesty can better serve the world's struggling people, where great inequalities exist in first-world and third-world nations.

Black Panther is timely, tackling race and gender at a time of global "wokeness." It is full of heroic actions, superhero powers, and science fantasy technology. The music, the visuals, and the action sequences carry the audience along. The acting seamlessly presents believable characters who might have turned cartoonish or indulgent. Instead, they shine (Travers, 2018). They are all multidimensional and thinking, reflecting, interacting beings. The audience is transported to a world more real than the black mirror. It adores its warriors, admires its king, and even weeps for the villain.

Much has already been written about this epic film, in which superhero action adventure becomes art: It is recognized for evoking a "haunting emotional response" (Henderson, 2018), for its political timeliness, and for breaking the "binary" on good and evil, on gender-roles, and on race (Dargis, 2018). Afrofuturism becomes real; Wakanda is what might have happened if Western Civilization had not built its wealth on slavery. While the "El Dorado" of Vibranium-rich Wakanda is unrealistic, many aspects of multi-cultural techno-driven Wakanda are not. This is one factor that draws viewers into *Black Panther*, not the power of the herb-transformed king, nor the super-charged action sequences or car chases. Why does the Afrofuturistic world of Wakanda speak so deeply to its audience? Authenticity. While the film adheres to many superhero Hollywood conventions, it presents a culture with its origin story intact and in which the hero's journey is real (Campbell, 2008; Donat, 2003). While not perfect, Wakanda seems real. Its authenticity comes from many sources. Clearly, the careful casting, the award-winning production and costume design ("*Black Panther* Awards," 2019; Watercutter, 2019) and the inclusive and forward-looking music score (Burlingame, 2018; Pearce, 2018) play a role.

Two features of *Black Panther* that contribute to this authenticity are myth and language. The film has a double opening, one myth and another, a hard reality. First, a Wakandan child, presumably T'Challa, the future Black Panther, asks his Baba about his people.

The discovery of the powers of Vibranium, and the power it gives to the first Black Panther, lead the people of the region to develop a culture that explores its properties. The different tribes coalesce into Wakanda, with an uneasy association with one outlier group, the Jabari, who embrace Hanuman instead of Bast, the panther goddess. These borrowings from global cultures resonate well. The Black Panther essentially becomes an avatar of Bast, the Egyptian goddess who defends the pharaoh. The Jabaris' affiliation with Hanuman reflects their cultural isolation from other Wakandans except in extreme need, but also aligns with the trickster features of M'Baku, their present leader, and his loyalty to Wakanda, even after generations of isolation in the snow country of the mountains of Wakanda. Drawing on world religions and mythologies, Wakanda's culture recognizes features of donor cultures as it builds its own creation myth centered on the appreciation of Vibranium as a gift, referred to as *isipho* in Xhosa-inspired Wakandan.

The Wakandan creation story has elements of the Garden of Eden. Men become aware of who they are and their possibilities after eating the special flower. It represents knowledge, as does the fruit eaten by Adam and Eve (Genesis 3). Its special powers also suggest the fruit of the Tree of Life, which Adam and Eve are prevented from eating, lest they become more god-like and evade death. The Black Panther is not immortal, but very nearly so, as the plant heals the king and all who come into contact with its special properties. However, instead of being driven out of Eden by their special knowledge of this powerful plant, the people of Wakanda harness the source of the plant's power, Vibranium, to create a world where knowledge and prosperity is extended to all within the dome protecting this Utopia from the outside world.

The special flower of Wakanda may have more in common with the magical flower found and then lost by the Sumerian king Gilgamesh on his journey back to Uruk, returning to his people after meeting the Mesopotamian Noah, Utnapishtim (*The Epic of Gilgamesh*).

Gilgamesh describes the flower as "a plant against decay, ... by which a man can attain his survival" (*Gilgamesh,* Tablet XI, Kovacs translation, 1989). In *Black Panther*, Wakanda is also reminiscent of Dilmun, the garden where Utnapishtim and his wife live, a place where valuable minerals have become subsumed into the plants and fruits of the earth. However, the valuable mineral of Wakanda is different from the decorative lapis lazuli, carnelian, rubies, hematite, and emeralds (*Gilgamesh*, Tablet IX). Instead, it is powers of Vibranium that infuse much of Wakanda.

In a reversal of the Eden myth, there is no god that evicts mankind once humans realize the power present in Eden. The awakened Wakandans remain in their paradise and prevent the rest of the world from realizing the possibilities offered by the plant and the Vibranium that it evolved from. They have usurped Eden and become like gods, albeit ones who hesitate to venture into the chaos of the rest of the world, specifically the chaos of the late twentieth and early twenty-first centuries.[1]

In a second opening, we see the violence and injustice of the outside world as experienced by one of the Wakandan War Dogs, spies who keep track of political and militaristic powers outside of Wakanda, presumably to maintain its secure isolation. A Black child in a ghetto looks into the sky and sees evidence of the myth his father has shared with him, that another place exists with futuristic technolo-

---

[1]   What other myths and cultural references could intertwine in the Wakandan cosmos? Perhaps the epic of the original lion king, Sundiata (Son Jara), whose mother was identified by a cat and who is born covered in hair, like a cat, contributes to the story of the Black Panther (Niane, 2016), or his great nephew, the famous Mansa Musa. The alternative narrative of African history and the diaspora also suggests such influential figures as Ghanaian Kwame Nkrumah or Jamaican Marcus Garvey.
Regarding the heart-shaped Vibranium-infused herb, it would be remiss to omit the parallels of cannabis use among some Rastafarians to connect with their ancestors, which is one effect of the Wakandan herb, although not the one that drives the most of the film. The ability to journey to the ancestral plane is a temporary aftereffect of the immediate ingestion of the herb, while the enhanced strength, heightened senses, and healing powers remain.

gy, where Blacks control their own destiny. By the time the child reaches his father's side, he has been killed by his brother T'Chaka, the Wakandan king and current Black Panther (played by Atandwa Kani as a young man and the legendary John Kani as the older king). The king's War Dog brother embraces his role as Black militant so thoroughly that he is willing to do anything to overthrow the racist oppression in America. He has even betrayed Wakanda in order to finance the arming of his American brothers. Prince N'Jobu (played by Sterling K. Brown) has revealed the secret of Wakandan isolation and wealth to a White South African arms dealer, and truly soulless villain, Ulysses Klaue (played by Andy Serkis). Myth is played out again. A brother renounces his birthright as Wakandan for a more immediate gain, the ability to respond to American racial violence. N'Jobu ideologically rejects his nation's isolationism, but his embrace of violence and betrayal engenders a new existential threat to Wakanda, after his son, N'Jadaka evolves into Erik Killmonger, played by Michael B. Jordan.

While the immediacy of sibling conflict ends with N'Jobu's death, his death fails to address the root cause of the conflict, isolationism in the face of injustice. The inflexibility of King T'Chaka leads to an unforgivable betrayal and perhaps plays a role in his own assassination years later. The abandonment of the child, an innocent in the ideological conflict of the brothers, remains a dark secret, a festering wound, and its own kind of betrayal. What becomes of the abandoned child is also largely predictable. He finds a way to return to Wakanda to reclaim the inheritance he was denied, his worldview further hardened by the violence resulting from racial and economic inequality, mastering the corrupt rules of the military industrial hegemony of the West, specifically the United States. As CIA Agent Ross (played by Martin Freeman) acknowledges, "He's one of ours" (*Black Panther*, 01:11:34).[2]

---

[2]   All timestamps come from *Black Panther.*

These two stories, the myth of a paradise untouched by the outside world and immune to its troubles and the desire of an abandoned child to reclaim his birthright, set the stage for the central action of *Black Panther*. The sins of the fathers are inherited by their sons in a world tearing itself apart with socio-economic injustice, racism, religious intolerance, and unashamed greed. One son struggles to maintain the Wakandan status quo, that is, isolationism with cautious forays into the outside world. The other, now a formidable warrior in his own right, seeks a way to return to Wakanda and realize an even more audacious version of his father's vision of using Wakanda's wealth to settle past debts.

From a theological perspective, perhaps the original sin of Wakanda is isolationism, the antithesis of engagement and community, but also a more understandable original sin as compared to that of colonialism and enslavement. However, even the deceased Black Panther, T'Chaka, when confronted by his son, T'Challa, on the Ancestral Plane, admits he "chose to omit" a truth, the existence of N'Jobu's son, N'Jadaka, who becomes Killmonger (01:37:01-01:37:07). Earlier, when confronted by T'Challa, Zuri, once the king's spy on his own brother and now the spiritual leader of Wakanda, confirms the abandonment of N'Jadaka: "We had to maintain the lie" (01:07:31-01:07:36).

What kind of a lie is Wakanda? In many ways, it is the paradise the father describes to his son in the opening scene. It is a complex futuristic world where economic prosperity seems to reign and the inequality and unjust distribution of resources plaguing the outside world is absent. There may be an overly simplistic representation of diversity in the film, as each "tribe" is assigned one sector of the Wakandan economy. However, we recognize great swathes of nations can be primarily fueled by one industry such as California's Silicon Valley, the American Midwest farm belt, and Texas oil and gas production. It is not too farfetched to imagine sectors of Wakanda represented by caste-like regional powers.

Another attractive aspect of Wakanda is its apparent absence of most aspects of gender inequality. The Queen Mother (played Angela Bassett) remains on the inner cabinet after the death of her husband. The representatives and speakers of some tribes include women. The War Dog spies include women who take on missions to disrupt abuses of African people where needed. Nakia, the Back Panther's (former) love interest (played by Lupita Nyong'o) enters the film on a mission to foil the abduction of girls and young women by a paramilitary force modeled after Boko Haram. The most fierce and capable warriors are the all-female Dora Milaje, who protect the throne. Perhaps these warriors are modeled on the Dahomey guardians of the King of Benin, as suggested in Coleman (2018, citing Serbin, 2014). Black Panther reaches back to pre-colonial African history, in which in some areas, females were accorded high status.

In some ways, Wakanda is a part of Africa as imagined by John Henrik Clarke and others, whose writings point to an alternative Africa, one that escaped colonialism and cultural imperialism (Acree, 2015). However, Wakanda is ruled by a monarchy, a disappointing anachronism, but true to the Marvel Comics origin story; the sacred herb can induce coma and death in those who are not of royal blood, presumably reflecting a genetic anomaly that can synergize the power of the plant. While the superhero in *Black Panther* may appear a throwback to chauvinism, the Black Panther bears a lot of responsibility and relies on a gender-neutral inner council for guidance. If anything, as played by the regal Chadwick Boseman, kingship inhibits T'Challa's power, rather than feeds it.[3]

With its Vibranium-fueled technology and science, Wakanda is the Harlem Renaissance on steroids. But Wakanda is also Africa unspoiled, with a diverse cast from the diaspora and the indigenous celebrating its strengths and diversities. This diversity cements the vision of Wakanda as not just one people, but several united. The

---

[3] Elsewhere, in the Marvel Comics Universe, T'Challa's sister Shuri becomes the Black Panther (Black Panther vol. 5, #1–2, April–May 2009).

strengths that the cast members bring to the film never wane. The Xhosa dialog provides authenticity, as does the choice to use varieties of African English as a lingua franca. While an African variety of the language of a colonizer makes *Black Panther* accessible to a global audience, the decision to use particular varieties provides distinctions among cast members and allows Wakandans to take ownership of their linguistic choices (Harris, 2018).

The fortuitous choice to make Xhosa the home language of Wakanda is due to the South African actor John Kani, who played the role of King T'Chaka in an earlier Marvel Universe film (*Captain America: Civil War*). *Black Panther* director Ryan Coogler and primary language coach, Beth McGuire, endorse this earlier decision (Harris, 2018). The addition of Xhosa adds authenticity to scenes establishing Wakandan identity: Xhosa establishes kinship, reinforces ritual and tradition, and plays a role in negotiating status and in excluding non-group members. Without a distinct African home language, the use of English as a lingua franca would fall flat.

Examples of Xhosa as language of ritual abound. In the ceremony to recognize T'Challa as king, everyone exhorts each other with the call to continue onward ("phambili"). Similarly, Wakandans praise the ancestors in Xhosa. When T'Challa visits the Ancestral Plane for a reunion with his deceased father, they begin their conversation in Xhosa. Only one English adjective occurs in the initial dialog, when T'Challa says ("andiyo ready, Baba" 'I am not ready, Baba') as he reestablishes his relationship with his father whose unforeseen assassination has left him feeling bereft and inadequate (00:31:39-00:31:41). However, once the conversation veers towards reigning a sovereign nation, both men speak in English.

One of the clearest examples of the effect of augmenting the dialog with Xhosa occurs in the second opening, in Oakland, CA, where King T'Chaka confronts his younger brother, Prince N'Jobu, over betraying Wakanda. First T'Chaka offers N'Jobu an opportunity to reconcile by addressing him as "Baby Brother" in Xhosa (00:4:33). However, he switches to English when N'Jobu fails disclose his involvement with the attack on Wakanda and the theft of Vibranium. This switch to English seems to repudiate his earlier affirmation of a special relationship with his younger brother. The king switches back to Xhosa to direct Zuri, another War Dog, to "tell him [Prince N'Jobu] who you are," underscoring his and Zuri's (James') identity as true Wakandans (00:53:21-00:53:40).

Using Xhosa to negotiate identity and to exclude also occurs when T'Challa catches up with Klaue in Buson, Korea. He calls him a murderer ("umbulali"), denying him humanity with the use of an exclusionary language. However, the rest of the world is watching, as Nakia and Okoye remind him, when they catch up with him just as he is ready to kill Klaue (00:53:21-00:53:40). Their use of Xhosa reminds T'Challa that his desire for revenge is balanced by the need to protect the secrets of Wakanda.

The scenes in Korea also illustrate another use of Xhosa, a more obvious one, where the little-known language of Wakanda (Xhosa) acts as a secret code for T'Challa, Nakia, and Okye. They use Xhosa to protect their insider identities from others, first from the thugs with the mercenary Klaue and then later from the American operatives, including Agent Ross. Okoye reassures him that she understands English "when she wants to," switching from the Xhosa she has been speaking with T'Challa in order to exclude Ross (00:54:58-00:55:00).

One interesting use of language is when Okoye refuses to go with Nakia, Shuri, and the Queen Mother as they flee from the new Black Panther, N'Jadaka/Erik Killmonger (01:22:30-01:23:45). Okoye thanks Nakia in Xhosa for secreting the queen and princess away. This personalizes their close relationship with the royal family and with each other. Yet, they have very different statuses and different interpretations of what it means to serve Wakanda. When Nakia tells

Okoye that they "should get to them immediately," Okoye refuses in Xhosa. As the general of the royal guard, she follows formal rules for governing Wakanda: a man of royal blood has defeated a king in ritual combat. She emphasizes the justness of her choice with Xhosa, and her insider status, compared with Nakia, who has chosen missions outside as a War Dog spy.

Nakia's and Okoye's continuing conversation, while entirely in English, is also linguistically significant because their linguistic choices illustrate how word choice and parataxis negotiate meaning and force the viewer to reflect on their different conceptions of loyalty. Nakia wants to "overthrow" Killmonger, but Okoye says she is "loyal to that throne, no matter who sits on it." When she questions Nakia's loyalty to Wakanda, Nakia redefines loyalty as "love." When Okoye says she intends to "serve" her country, Nakia says she will "save" her country. The specific linguistic choices they make as they reformulate notions of loyalty and duty provide a window into their roles and their characters.

Of course, the majority of the dialog in *Black Panther* is in English, more specifically African English varieties. That Wakanda would employ a lingua franca fits its identity a nation hiding in plain sight. Wakanda can negotiate its outward identity without revealing much of its true nature. The choice of a dominant African lingua franca, African English, or more accurately, varieties of African English, also allows Wakandan War Dogs to move largely unrecognized.

Perhaps one reason *Black Panther* has largely escaped the charge of cultural appropriation is that its cast includes Africans and members of the African diaspora with clear cultural and linguistic ties to Africa and African English varieties. Dialect coach Beth McGuire describes developing dialects for the central characters as "original primary accents fold[ed] into another accent" (Harris, 2018). The family of Daniel Kaluuya (W'Kabi, guardian of the border) recently immigrated to the UK from Uganda. Danai Gurira's family is from

Zimbabwe. Letitia Wright is from British Guyana. Lupita Nyong'o is able to use her primary accent with an overlay of Xhosa; Nakia has established her identity as a "Kenyan heiress" in the underground markets of Korea (00:43:00).

The linguistic skills of more removed members of the African diaspora are not to be underestimated. Chadwick Bosman plays the Black Panther. A native of South Carolina, he has already played a Supreme Court justice (Thurgood Marshall), a musician (James Brown), and an athlete (Jackie Robinson). Bosman explains his choice to model his Wakandan English after African varieties instead of an educated colonial variety: "He's the ruler of a nation. And if he's the ruler of a nation, he has to speak to his people" (qtd. in Guglielmo, 2018). The king's variety has to reflect his alignment with his people and not the colonizers he interacts with at the United Nations and other outside venues. Bosman clarifies the ideology behind his choice: "If it's supposed to not have been conquered – which means that advancement has happened without colonialism tainting it, poisoning the well of it, without stopping it or disrupting it – then there's no way he would speak with a European accent" (qtd. in Guglielmo, 2018). That is, the African variety is the new standard for Wakanda, and by extension, for Africa. There is no need to aspire to the dialect of a colonizer.

One of the more interesting Wakandan varieties is the dialect spoken by the Jabari. Winston Duke, from Trinidad and Tobago, is their leader, M'Baku. M'Baku's West African Vernacular English is particularly interesting. His challenge to T'Challa is preceded by this speech: "We have watched and listened from the mountains! We have watched with disgust as your technological advancements have been overseen by a child! Who scoffs at tradition! And now you want to hand the nation over to this prince who could not keep his own father safe. Mmm? We will not have it. I said, we will not have it, oh!" (23:40-24:20). This speech reflects the formal style, deliberative repetition, and elevated vocabulary of Benue-Congo influenced varieties. The emphatic "oh" at the end of an exclamation validates his disapproval, as might be expected in Nigerian Standard English.

No discussion of English varieties in *Black Panther* would be complete without reflecting on Michael B. Jordan's speech. His African American Vernacular English (AAVE) is appropriate for someone who grew up in the streets of Oakland, CA, but must also be construed as a conscious choice to use a style that disassociates him from more standard American English, a variety he must also control, as a graduate of Annapolis (the United States Naval Academy) and a graduate student at MIT. In his speech to the Wakandan advisors to T'Challa, Killmonger, or N'Jadaka, says "It's about two billion people all over the world that looks like us" (01:14:26-01:14:29). Here the nonreferential "it" substitutes for existential "there," a common feature of AAVE. Similarly, verbal inflection adds aspect and emphasis rather than grammatical feature matching ("people that … looks like …") (Wolfram, 2004; Poplack and Tagliamonte, 2004). Killmonger uses "ain't" when challenging T'Challa's rejection of a pan-African worldview ("So ain't all people your people?"), another feature of AAVE (01:1456-01:14:57). This usage marks his oppositional identity to acting white through speaking in a standard white American English variety (Fordham and Ogbu, 1986).

Interestingly, Killmonger must have some competence in Wakandan. He responds to W'Kabi's question of his identity at the border and T'Challa's command to speak ("Thetha!") (01:13:45). When the leader of the River Tribe askes him name in Xhosa, he replies in Xhosa: "Ndingu N'Jadaka, unyana ka N'Jobu." ("I am N'Jadaka, son of N'Jobu") (01:15:49-01:15:43). Some of the complexities of Killmonger's character are reflected in his style of speaking. Although he is a member of the American military and intelligence elite, he chooses the style of the oppressed and less educated, while still using Wakandan to show his rightful claim to challenge T'Challa for the throne.

Of course, one of *Black Panther's* appeals is that it is a superhero action film. But even this is tempered by the more complex central story. Erik Killmonger seeks to restore his father's vision of Wakanda liberating African people globally, at any cost. He sells his soul to those who would destroy his own people, both Wakandan and other oppressed peoples, specifically, to the unprincipled corrupt Ulysses Klaue. Klaue may be clever enough to steal and escape from punishment, but his undoing comes when he underestimates Killmonger, admitting he thought he was "just another crazy American" (01:03:40-01:03:45). While destroying entrenched remnants of colonial oppression may have noble features, Killmonger is also full of desire for revenge.

Killmonger's visit to the Ancestral Plane, after drinking the Vibranium herb infusion, reveals him still partly a child, unable to move forward in spite of his many accomplishments. Sometimes he speaks the truth, but it is a truth tinged with bitterness and violence. At times, Killmonger shines with the cynical intelligence of an evil twin of the trickster. When he confronts the ill-fated museum specialist, he says "How do you think your ancestors got these? You think they paid a fair price? Or did they take it, like they took everything else?" (00:16:36-00:16:43). He kills to reclaim Wakandan heritage, and kills again to reach the forbidden land. Yet, even T'Challa, the Black Panther, recognizes he is within rights to demand a challenge to the throne. T'Challa has inherited the culmination of millennia of isolation and decades of deceit, and he accepts his inherited responsibilities.

The ritual combat with Killmonger, T'Challa's inferred death, and his Lazarus-like return provide opportunities for the complexities of key characters to be illustrated. W'Kabi, played by Daniel Kaluuya, reveals his own desire for revenge for an earlier border attack which killed his parents. Killmonger's gift of the dead Klaue feeds that desire and allows him to consider a different Wakanda, one which can be open about its military prowess, instead of concealing it behind a defensive wall. As leader of the border guard, this alternate view feeds his sense of purpose and expertise better than hiding in secrecy. Nakia, the Black Panther's ex, has seen the outside world and knows what Killmonger's actions can lead to, not a reversal of centuries of violence and oppression, but a more intense violence perhaps leading to global Armageddon. Shuri, the Black Panther's sister, expertly and smartly played by Letitia Wright, also knows the dangers of allowing the power of Vibranium to be misused. These actors struggle with their responses to Killmonger's takeover. Fortunately, Okoye's loyalty to the throne and the protocols determining its occupant allow a return of her allegiance to T'Challa; the ritual combat is not over, as neither Killmonger nor T'Challa ceded the fight and neither is dead.

I suspect that one aspect of *Black Panther's* appeal is that its myths are not the result of alien encounters or alternative universes. To be believable, myth must be at the boundary of human experience. The linguistic and cultural choices made in the production of *Black Panther* accomplish this. Its myths reflect the inner psychology of men with power to control their own destinies and defend their world and a vision of a real place, unspoiled Africa. The same inner struggles of human history exist: sibling conflict, the return of the abandoned child, the loyalty to ideals, and ultimately the willingness to sacrifice and to change, to be reborn.

Initially, T'Challa rejects looking outward except in matters of state security. T'Challa's second chance to direct his nation's destiny follows a different path, once he sees the enormity of the consequences of the original choice. This second chance is afforded him as a result of his rebirth, in terms of Joseph Campbell's "Hero's Journey." While Wakanda is in controlled chaos as Killmonger plans an empire in which the sun never sets on Wakandan rule, three women, and Agent Ross, attempt a desperate plan to defeat Killmonger. Nakia has saved a single herb flower to offer the Jabari ruler, M'Baku. The Jabari army offers what she perceives as the only hope for

Wakanda. M'Baku's dialog with these women is memorable, as is his silencing of Ross, but more remarkable are his honesty and loyalty to Wakanda, even though his people live afar, in the mountains. He reveals that T'Challa lives, albeit in a hypothermic coma. He repays a debt to T'Challa, who returns, after confronting his dead father a second time.

Revived by the sacred herb, and aided by his sister's ingenuity and the now justly unconstrained Dora Milaje, T'Challa returns to fight Killmonger and the forces loyal to him. What wisdom does the Black Panther bring back from the dead? That Wakanda's continued isolationism is a refusal of the great struggle, the obligation to act wisely and inclusively when blessed with power and abundance. But first, the Black Panther must restore order within his own house. The ensuing battle between the forces loyal to the new king, N'Jadaka, or Killmonger, and those loyal to T'Challa does not disappoint. However, these are not the forces of good and evil, but the forces of the seduced and the desperately brave.

The allegiances of Wakandans are tested until the final flight of weapons to the outside is stopped, the Dora Milaje subdue the Border Security forces, and the Jabari join the Black Panther to reject outsiders deciding the fate of Wakanda. M'Baku's entrance to the battle assures the ground battle is won. Shuri and Agent Ross manage to destroy the last outgoing ship. The continuing ritual combat, magnified by the strength of the herb, continues in the heart of the Vibranium mountain. The rightful king eventually defeats the would-be usurper, all the while lamenting the loss of the child now turned enemy. The fatally wounded Killmonger shows the depth of his tormented identity. In this scene, the audience recognizes that the child in the opening scene was N'Jadaka, not T'Challa. Killmonger reveals how the injustices of the world, or at least the injustices of America, have distorted his worldview: "My pop said Wakanda was the most beautiful thing he ever seen. He promised he was gonna show it to me one day. You believe that? Kid from Oakland, running around believing in fairy tales" (1:56:17-1:19:39) (Tassi, 2018). Even though T'Challa suggests he might still be saved, Killmonger rejects this, fearing loss of liberty. He refuses to consider what his life has always rejected, the captivity of the Black man.

Why will *Black Panther* remain one of the most important films of its era, not just a top-grossing, award-winning blockbuster? Because it is a truly amazing superhero film that tells a timeless and epic story, and does it well. The story arc, the acting, the set and costume designs – all create a believable world, but more significantly, a world the audience wants to believe is real or could be real. We want the world promised in the post-credit scenes, a world where there is enough abundance for all and the sources of poverty and conflict can be defeated globally, a world where there is hope and opportunity for children in impoverished urban ghettos. The superhero-loving audience will welcome sequels, but it is hard to imagine a film that could satisfy so deeply. The messages of this *Black Panther* hero's journey appeal to our better selves. "Wakanda forever!"

Postscript:

The year 2020 has seen many challenges and much turmoil, coupled with much loss. One loss is the remarkable actor Chadwick Boseman, the Black Panther. Unbeknownst to his audience and fellow actors, he portrayed a noble figure, all the while engaged in his own battle with cancer. He left us way too early.

References

Acree, Eric Kofi. 2015. "John Henrik Clarke: Historian, Scholar, and Teacher." John Henrik Clarke Africana Library, Cornell University. Retrieved from https://africana.library.cornell.edu/africana/clarke/index.html.

Black Panther. 2018. Directed by Ryan Coogler, written by Ryan Coogler and Joe Robert Cole, based on Marvel Comics by Stan Lee and Jack Kirby, Marvel Studios.

"*Black Panther* Awards." 2019. *IMDb,* IMDb.com, Inc. Retrieved from https://www.imdb.com/title/tt1825683/awards.

Burlingame, Jon. 2018, Feb. 14. "*Black Panther* Composer Infuses Score with Trove of African Sounds." *Variety*, Variety Media, LLC. Retrieved from https://variety.com/2018/artisans/production/black-panther-score-1202697385/.

Campbell, Joseph. 2008. *The Hero with a Thousand Faces*. New World Library, 3rd ed.

Coleman, Arica L. 2018, Feb. 22. "There's a True Story Behind *Black Panther's* Strong Women. Here's Why That Matters." *Time*. Retrieved from http://time.com/5171219/black-panther-women-true-history/.

Dargis, Manohla. 2018, Feb. 6. "Review: 'Black Panther' Shakes Up the Marvel Universe." *The New York Times*. Retrieved from https://www.nytimes.com/2018/02/06/movies/black-panther-review-movie.html.

Donat, Peter, et al. 2003. *Joseph Campbell: The Hero's Journey*. New York: Wellspring Media.

The Epic of Gilgamesh, translated by Maureen Gallery Kovacs. 1989. Stanford University Press. Electronic edition available at *The Academy of Ancient Texts.* Retrieved from http://www.ancienttexts.org/library/mesopotamian/gilgamesh/tab1.htm.

Fordham, Signithia and John Ogbu. 1986. "Black Students' School Success: Coping with the Burden of 'Acting White'." *Urban Review* 18: 176–206.

Guglielmo, Connie. 2918, Feb. 8. "*Black Panther* Rules Marvel's World. Literally." *CNET*. CBS Interactive. Inc. Retrieved from https://www.cnet.com/news/black-panther-chadwick-boseman-marvel-king-of-wakanda/.

Harris, Aisha. 2018, Feb. 18. "*Black Panther's* Dialect Coach on Wakanda's Regional Accents and Prepping Actors." (Interview with Beth McGuire). *Slate*. Retrieved from https://slate.com/culture/2018/02/an-interview-with-black-panthers-dialect-coach.html.

Henderson, Odie. 2018, Mar. 8. "*Black Panther* Movie Review and Summary." *RogerEbert.com*. Retrieved from https://www.rogerebert.com/reviews/black-panther-2018.

Kendi, Ibram X. 2019, Jan. 13. "The Day 'Shithole' Entered the Presidential Lexicon." *The Atlantic*. Retrieved from https://www.theatlantic.com/politics/archive/2019/01/shithole-countries/580054/.

Niane, D. T. 2016. *Sundiata: An Epic of Old Mali*, Longman African Writers Series. Pearson, rev. ed.

Pearce, Sheldon. 2018, Feb. 12. "*Black Panther:* The Album." *Pitchfork.* Retrieved from https://pitchfork.com/reviews/albums/various-artists-black-panther-the-album/.

Poplack, Shana, and Sali Tagliamonte. 2004. "Back to the Present: Verbal -s in the (African American) English Diaspora. *The Legacy of Non-Standard Colonial English: The Study of Transported Dialects*, ed. by R. Hickey, pp. 203-223. Cambridge: Cambridge University Press. Retrieved from http://www.sociolinguistics.uottawa.ca/shanapoplack/pubs/articles/PoplackTagliamonte2004.pdf.

Serbin, Sylvia 2014. *The Women Soldiers of Dahomey,* UNESCO. Retrieved from https://en.unesco.org/womeninafrica/sites/womeninafrica/files/pdf/The%20Women%20Soldiers%20of%20Dahomey_Women%20in%20African%20History_Comic%20Strip_0.pdf.

Tassi, Paul. 2018, Feb. 19. "Five Things You Probably Missed in *Black Panther*." *Forbes.* Forbes Media LLC. Retrieved from https://www.forbes.com/sites/forbes-finds/2019/07/01/stylish-fourth-of-july-home-decor/#30e5d89f5cd2.

Travers, Peter. 2018, Feb. 6. "Review: Marvel's History-Making Superhero Movie a Masterpiece." *Rolling Stone.* Retrieved from https://www.rollingstone.com/movies/movie-reviews/black-panther-review-marvels-history-making-superhero-movies-a-masterpiece-198071/.

Watercutter, Angela. 2019, Feb. 25. "*Black Panther's* Oscar Wins Made History." *Wired.* Retrieved from https://www.wired.com/story/black-panthers-oscar-wins-made-history/.

Wolfram, Walt. 2004. "The Grammar of Urban African American Vernacular English." (Research funded by NSF, HHS, and William C. Friday Endowment at North Carolina State University). Available at *Semantic Scholar*. Retrieved from https://pdfs.semanticscholar.org/8c27/7045aff1335d6612c83206109a41a40bcf6d.pdf?_ga=2.237723017.869968852.1562058585-51909198.1562058585.

Marie Hartkopf

The Power of Language: How Littlefinger and Tyrion Lannister Use Language to Gain Power

I

One of the predominant themes of the fantasy television series *Game of Thrones* (*GoT*) is the possession of power or respectively the struggle to achieve such power. Within the world of *Game of Thrones*, power is most evidently represented through the Iron Throne, upon which the king of Westeros is seated. This rather uncomfortable seat fashioned out of a thousand melted swords is arguably the most contested object in the entirety of Westeros and even plays an important role in the lands to the East, a continent called Essos. As the title of the series suggests, it essentially all boils down to who wins the throne and rules the kingdom as the most powerful person.

But what is power, and how can it be achieved? The political economist and sociologist Max Weber defined that "power […] is the probability that one actor within a social relationship will be in a position to carry out his own will despite resistance, regardless of the basis on which this probability rests" (53). He then goes on to subdivide power into three components or means of enforcement. The first is 'authority', i.e. "the threat and application of physical force on the part of the administrative staff" (54). The second variation is 'influence', i.e. "exerting influence on the government of a political organization; especially at the appropriation, expropriation, redistribution or allocation of the powers of government" (54) and lastly, psychic 'coercion' is used for instance by a church through "distributing or denying religious benefits" (54).

Since the society of *Game of Thrones* resembles a medieval society with kings and queens, lords and ladies, power is primarily distributed through means such as societal status and wealth as well as physical strength, which can all be achieved by a fortunate birth into one of the noble Houses (e.g. Houses Stark, Baratheon, Lannister, etc.), which hold a certain amount of power within the realm of Westeros. These Houses represent authority and usually have the necessary means to influence or even coerce others into doing something beneficial for their own interests. However, there exists another, more subtle, expression of power that is utilized by a small number of characters within the narrative, who might otherwise be rather disadvantaged. This other source of power, according to the character Petyr 'Littlefinger' Baelish[1] is knowledge.

The importance of knowledge in relation to power is evidenced by Stephen Schneck, who quotes a popular aphorism by philosopher Francis Bacon that goes "scientia potestas est," which translates to "knowledge is power" (27). He asserts from this aphorism that "knowledge is the vehicle to achieve liberation" (27). Thus, knowledge seems to have a rather important function in the struggle for power. Accordingly, it becomes clear that power does not only have a physical manifestation, but can also be achieved by other non-forceful means.

These two variations of power are contrasted within the series in a scene between Littlefinger and Queen Cersei Lannister. Littlefinger confronts Cersei, who is escorted by knights of the Kingsguard (i.e. the royal guard). In the ensuing conversation, Littlefinger claims that "knowledge is power." Cersei reacts by giving commands to the Kingsguard and asking them to "seize him", upon which they grab Littlefinger and hold a knife to his throat. Cersei then goes on to demonstrate her power over the Kingsguard by commanding them to let Littlefinger go again, and then she claims, "power is power" ("The North Remembers"). In this particular instance, Cersei's physical power has the upper hand, as she could have seized

---

[1]   This character will henceforth be referred to as Littlefinger.

Littlefinger without struggle. Yet, there is a valuable truth to Littlefinger's statement that knowledge is power.

He is a character of insignificant birth from a remote part of Westeros, which, according to the laws and customs of Westeros, would not make him a very important man and certainly not someone holding a high position. And yet, he has managed to rise up in ranks throughout his life, ending up as a member of the Small Council and Master of Coins at the beginning of the television series, meaning that he has direct influence on the King and is involved in the decision making. How is this rise to power possible, when Cersei is to be believed that only "power is power"?

In order to assess this, it is important to first gaze at knowledge and its true significance for power in order to get a deeper understanding of how Littlefinger, as well as other disadvantaged characters, are able to climb to power. In general, "[knowledge] is a production of human statements" (Schneck 18), which infers that knowledge is connected to language. It requires a certain form of language production in order to be manifested, for example in the form of speech or writing. Furthermore, humans rely on language in order to communicate information, and ultimately societies are built on language (Coulmas 56). If humans had no means to collect and preserve knowledge, our societies would be much more rudimental, since "purposeful intelligent behavior may accelerate evolution" (Savage-Rumbaugh et al. 911). Additionally, Savage-Rumbaugh et al. put forward that "culture constructs the structure of our consciousness so that we […] are able to share experiences" (911). Only through the sharing of experiences does knowledge transcend the obstacle of time and can be passed on from generation to generation. This shows that language plays an essential role in the construction of a society and that the idea of knowledge is inherently connected to language.

Knowledge, in this sense, can be seen as an extension of language. It is achieved by usage of language in a way that yields information and subsequently empowers the speaker. Referring back to Weber's definition of power, power is connected to means of coercion and influence, both of which rely on language and discourse to be enforced. These variations of power can be attributed to certain characters within *Game of Thrones*, who use coercion and influence, sometimes in extreme forms such as manipulation, in their striving for power.

How this plays out in the television series is most suitably displayed by the characters Littlefinger, as suggested above, and Tyrion Lannister, who has the advantage of being born into a noble family, but faces vast disadvantages due to the fact that he was born a dwarf. He admits that "if I'd been born a peasant, they might have left me in the woods to die" ("The Kingsroad"), showing that in his father's eyes, he is not worthy of having such a high status as a Lannister. What these two characters have in common is that despite their disadvantageous situations, they manage to climb to a position of power, or, in Tyrion's case, maintain that inherent power by using some form of knowledge enforced through their individual techniques of language command or manipulation. How they individually manage this will be seen in the following analyses of some of their dialogues and speeches within the series.

II

"Those who control discourse may indirectly control the minds of people" (van Dijk 10). Mind control in this instance is not understood as the literal sense which is often depicted in science-fiction stories (i.e. the literal telepathic control of one's mind) but more in the sense of manipulating the minds of others and making them do something simply by twisting their thoughts in a way that is beneficial to the person who enforces the 'mind control'.

If anyone in Westeros comes close to exerting this form of mind control, it is Littlefinger. As mentioned above, he was born into an insignificant family with rather low status and yet at the beginning of the television series, he is seated on the Small Council as Master of Coins, arguably one of the most powerful positions in Westeros, because he directly influences the king and manages his expenses. In the beginning of the series, the viewer sees him as a character who mostly acts in the background, never really taking center stage, and it quickly becomes clear that his true intentions are similarly hidden. He starts out as a small minor character, but over the course of the series he becomes more and more involved in the unfolding events and it becomes apparent to the viewer that Littlefinger is in fact one of the prime influencers in the society of Westeros, functioning as a sort of puppet master who easily controls his subjects and always comes out on top.

To Littlefinger, "chaos is a ladder" and he claims that life is all about the climb ("The Climb"), meaning the rise to power. Although he does not specifically mention the end of the figurative ladder, it is insinuated that his desired destination is to sit on the Iron Throne, i.e. to become the ruler of Westeros and be the most powerful person. These are rather large ambitions for a man of his insignificant background, but, as will be shown, he is actually efficient in this steady rise to power.

One of his biggest strengths is the manipulation of people while maintaining a certain pretense that his intentions are purely beneficial for his allies and for the realm. Seemingly all he does is in favor of the characters he helps out, but that this is actually not the case becomes evident over the course of the series. In fact, Littlefinger is likely the most egoistic and narcissistic character in the entire series, which is hinted at by means of his sigil, a mockingbird. Every great House in Westeros has a sigil, a certain animal or figurine that represents the House and functions as an identifier. The Lannisters for instance sport a lion, representing their strength, and the Starks have a direwolf, hinting at the pack mentality of the family and their Northern roots. Littlefinger deemed it necessary to create his own sigil, not wanting to be associated with anyone else. Incidentally, the scientific name of the mockingbird is "mimus polyglottus," which translates to "many-tongued mimic" as the bird mimics the sounds of other birds in nature (Tveten and Tveten 234). Similarly, Littlefinger easily 'mimics' the behavior of other characters, making them believe that they share the same intentions and ideologies. This is where his language command comes into play, as this mimicking of other characters is directly related to the way he articulates himself in certain situations, and it plays an important role in his ability of manipulation and 'mind control'.

Teun van Dijk claims that "'mind control' involves much more than just understanding text or talk, but also personal and social knowledge, previous experiences, personal opinions and social attitudes […]" (11). To successfully exert 'mind control' it is necessary to understand one's opponent as well as the cultural and societal context; these are all factors that Littlefinger knows and understands how to use. Language, similarly, is often directly related to social identities and social settings (Fairclough 17) and perhaps more than any other character (aside from Tyrion, as shown below), Littlefinger knows how to read people and their desires and how to use this to his advantage.

A prime example of Littlefinger's understanding of settings is a scene in which Littlefinger summons Catelyn Stark, who has just arrived in King's Landing in order to investigate the attempted murder of her son. Littlefinger finds her and brings her into one of his brothels (which he uses to make money but also to obtain information from his clients), which enrages Catelyn. However, he quickly reassures her by saying, "I meant no disrespect to you, of all people." He then explains, "no one will come looking for you here, isn't that what you wanted?" ("Lord Snow"). This brief dialogue indicates his game at work, as this dialogue happens briefly before he falsely informs Catelyn that the dagger that was used in the attempt to murder her son belonged to Tyrion Lannister. With this short dialogue, Littlefinger first appeals to the friendly relationship between Catelyn and himself, as they have grown up together ("you, of all people"). He then acknowledges her wish to stay undercover ("no one will come looking here") and finally appeals to her empathy ("I am truly sorry about the locale").

This shows that he portrays himself as a friend, who acts in her favor and only has her safety and well-being in mind, which ultimately leads Catelyn to trust him. As a result of this gained trust, she believes in his accusations and henceforth accuses Tyrion as responsible for the attempted murder of her son. As a viewer, you know that this accusation is false and that Tyrion is innocent, and yet Catelyn captures him anyway, which creates more chaos and strife in the realm, making the Starks and Lannisters direct enemies. Ultimately, this results in the brutal execution of her husband Ned Stark and splits the realm into war, creating exactly the chaos that Littlefinger strives for.

What is interesting is that Littlefinger is so successful because he does not simply impose his own will on other people, but instead digs deep into their inner desires and uses this to his advantage. John Edwards mentions that influence on someone else typically involves reciprocity and that "the person influenced is a captive of his or her own desires in regard to what is controlled by another" (16). This means that in order for the influence to work, the influencer needs to understand the opponent's desires and inner workings.

In the case of Catelyn, Littlefinger is aware that she is searching for a person responsible for the murder attempt, someone she can blame. He is also aware that Catelyn already blames the Lannister's for one murder, namely the murder of her sister's husband Jon Arryn, because Littlefinger was involved in the plot to kill Jon Arryn and the scheme to accuse the Lannisters of this murder. Thus, Littlefinger is aware of Catelyn's existing distrust of the Lannisters as well as her wish for justice and easily plants the idea in her mind that Tyrion Lannister is guilty.

He does something similar with Ned Stark a little later in the first season. In the episode "Cripples, Bastards, and Broken Things", Littlefinger and Ned walk along the gardens of the castle in King's Landing and Littlefinger claims that he works in Ned's interest on behalf of Catelyn ("I promised Cat that I'd help you"), which engenders a friendly relationship between the two characters. He then proceeds to inform Ned about the various spies at work in the castle, seeming to let Ned in on the secrecy surrounding them. This is essential, as it suggests to Ned that Littlefinger is actively helping him by pointing out that everyone has spies and is potentially plotting something. In this case, Littlefinger seems as though he acts in favor of Ned. Lastly, he establishes a form of trust by telling him vital information about Jon Arryn and the mystery surrounding his death. As a result, Ned remarks that perhaps he was wrong to distrust him, but Littlefinger replies: "Distrusting me was the wisest thing you've done since you climbed off your horse" ("Cripples, Bastards, and Broken Things"). This last exchange is particularly interesting, because this time Littlefinger uses the truth in order to manipulate Ned Stark by admitting that he is not to be trusted. Despite this warning, perhaps falling prey to reverse psychology, Ned does put his trust in Littlefinger because the information provided is of great help to Ned's investigation, but ultimately his trust in Littlefinger is his own demise, as Littlefinger betrays him and helps the Lannisters capture him and accuse him of treason, which eventually results in Ned Stark's death.

Again, Littlefinger works out Ned Stark's inner desires to use these against him and in his own favor. Ned's biggest character trait is his honor and Littlefinger knows that Ned would do anything to maintain his honor. This means that Ned would never accept the illegitimate Joffrey Baratheon as king and instead accepts the more perilous decision of supporting the late king Robert Baratheon's brother Stannis Baratheon, despite being aware of the Lannisters' strength. What Ned Stark underestimates is Cersei Lannister's ruthlessness and disregard for honor, and Littlefinger uses this quite stubborn mindset of Ned to undermine him, because he knows very well that it is more rational to support the powerful Lannisters and that Cersei would never willingly step down from her seat of power and would rather start a war than give up her crown.

These two scenes are just early examples of Littlefinger's manipulative power and influence by means of language in the form of dialogues with other more direct and transparent characters. They highlight his control of the discourse and the fact that his opponents do not have any chance of escaping his calculating influence, because he easily recognizes the individual's desires and inner workings and manipulates them in a way that is beneficial to himself and those who can aid him.

However, it is important to note that Littlefinger's understanding of language and his manipulative powers are not the only means by which he climbs to power. One of his predominant means of manipulation and influence is sexuality. He uses his brothels to obtain information from his clients, who become chatty when they are pleasured. On top of that, he uses his own sexuality to manipulate women, especially the sisters Catelyn Stark and Lysa Arryn, both of whom he grew up with. In Catelyn's case, he refers back to the love he once felt for her before she married Ned Stark and he uses this apparent love in order to gain her trust (as suggested above), and this extends to Catelyn's daughter Sansa, who becomes Littlefinger's new obsession and who trusts that he will help her (which results in her being sold to the Boltons).

With Lysa Arryn this works reversely, as she is the one who is in love with Littlefinger, and he uses her devotion to blatantly manipulate her. This is revealed in the fourth season, when Lysa says to

Littlefinger: "What wife would trust you the way I've trusted you? When you gave me those drops, and told me to pour them into Jon's wine, my husband's wine, when you told me to write a letter to Cat telling her it was the Lannisters?" ("First of His Name"). This refers all the way back to season one and the conflict between the Lannisters and the Starks. This event, the poisoning of Jon Arryn, can in fact be seen as the catalyst for the entire plot of the series, as it is the reason why Ned Stark came to King's Landing and what brought about the ensuing war. Later in the same scene, Lysa marries Littlefinger, resulting in him becoming Lord of the Vale, thus giving him another title and another increase in power. This shows that he knows well how to use sexuality and the physical desires of women as well as men in order to further manipulate other characters.

Throughout the series, he establishes himself as a chess player who moves his pieces (i.e. other characters) around the board to place them where he needs them to fulfill his plans. At the notion of power, the character Varys claims that "power resides where men believe it resides. It's a trick. A shadow on the wall" ("What Is Dead May Never Die"), and this perfectly suits Littlefinger's role. Nobody truly believes that he is powerful. He is, after all, just someone from a little-known House without any notable titles or armies. That is precisely his strength, though. Nobody ever accuses Littlefinger of being responsible for any of the events that happen, because he makes sure that there are always others to blame, often characters with higher status and more power. He talks people into doing things for him and then finds ways to stay in the background. And yet, he is indirectly responsible for almost all of the major events moving the plot forward (i.e. Jon Arryn's death, Tyrion's arrest, Ned's injury, Joffrey's death, Sansa's rape) and for causing strife and chaos in Westeros while he, in accordance to his statement that chaos is indeed a ladder, always makes it out on top, winning more and more titles. In this way, he makes it from Master of Coins to Lord of Harrenhal and subsequently to Lord Protector of the Vale and he almost gains power over the North as well by manipulating Sansa Stark.

His genius is summed up in a conversation he has with Sansa:

"Don't fight in the North or the South. Fight every battle, every-where, always, in your mind. Everyone is your enemy, everyone is your friend, every possible series of events is happening, all at once. Live that way, and nothing will surprise you. Everything that happens will be something that you've seen before." ("The Queen's Justice")

This again emphasizes his ability to read characters' intentions and to anticipate how they are going to react to the things he says to them. In understanding his conversational partners, he understands how to construct the narrative in a way that benefits him without seeming obvious. He understands the power of language and decep-tion and the inner desires of people, using this knowledge to realize his own visions and to steadily rise in power.

III

Tyrion Lannister, similar to Littlefinger, uses language and knowl-edge in order to rise to power, or in his case rather to maintain his power. As briefly mentioned above, Tyrion already has a certain amount of power as a result of his birth as a Lannister, one of the richest and most influential families in Westeros, but his dwarfism has made him an irrelevant figure in his father's eyes. He does not have his brother's strength nor does he desire an advantageous mar-riage like his sister, who married the king.

Instead, Tyrion turns to knowledge as his trait to set himself apart from others and he applies his knowledge in multiple occasions. One of his biggest strengths is to assess social situations and adapt his language accordingly, thus enabling him to converse at ease not only with noble men but also with peasants, sellswords like Bronn (i.e. swordsmen who can be bought to fight for someone) and even rudimental tribe folks such as the hill tribes he encounters after be-ing released from captivity in the Vale of Arryn.

This ability to literally talk himself out of perilous situations is what has kept him alive throughout the series and what continues to keep him in positions of power. Even though he loses this power numerous times (e.g. being captured by Catelyn, being imprisoned by Cersei, being exiled to Essos, being captured by a slave trader) he always seems to find his way back to power simply by talking and persuading people to help him. John Edwards puts forward that "beneath the specifics of language […] lies the psychologically deeper matter of identity" (19), meaning that language is always closely tied to one's identity and can be adapted accordingly.

Tyrion, as someone who has struggled with his own identity for so long, is deeply concerned with adapting to his situation and has found his strength in his own identity. In a conversation with the bastard Jon Snow, he lectures him, "Let me give you some advice, bastard. Never forget what you are. The rest of the world will not. Wear it like armor and it can never be used to hurt you" ("Winter Is Coming"). This indicates that Tyrion has come to terms with his disadvantage of being a dwarf and is using this in turn to make it his strength. Not only does he have a good grasp of his own identity, but he also understands other characters on a deeper level than most, being able to identify with them and dig deeper into their identity struggles.

The first example where this really becomes apparent is when he is imprisoned by Lysa Arryn (after Catelyn Stark's accusation) and is kept in a cell until he confesses his crime, i.e. the attempted murder of Catelyn's son. This puts Tyrion in a dilemma, because he is not guilty, hence he has nothing to confess, but he also knows that he won't get out of the cell without confessing. Instead, Tyrion assesses that the guard put in front of his cell is of a simple mind and he uses this in his favor. Tyrion engages the guard in a conversation and attempts to bribe him to release Tyrion: "Have you ever heard the phrase 'rich as a Lannister'? 'Course you have, you're a smart man. You know who the Lannisters are. I am a Lannister. Tyrion, son of

Tywin. Of course, you've also heard the phrase 'a Lannister always pays his debts'. If you deliver a message from me to Lady Arryn, I will be in your debt. I will owe you gold" ("A Golden Crown"). With this strategy, Tyrion gains the trust of the guard and is able to talk himself out of the dangerous situation. First, he manages to appeal to the guard's pride by calling him smart, giving the guard a sense of importance. Tyrion then uses his family name as a means of persuasion, knowing full well that his name is associated with power and wealth and the prospect of receiving Lannister gold. Tyrion's scheme works out, as the guard does bring the message to Lysa Arryn. He is brought forth to a court to confess and subsequently manages to walk away as a free man with the help of the sellsword Bronn.[2]

Not much later, he finds himself in another perilous situation when the hill tribes of the Vale attack Tyrion and Bronn. In a similar manner, he tries to persuade them by promising them gold and better armor, but it does not work out, as the hill tribes have no use for it. Accordingly, Tyrion goes one step further. "If you help us [...], I will not give you trinkets. I will give you this. [...] The Vale of Arryn. The Lords of the Vale have always spat upon the hill tribes. The Lords of the Vale want me dead. I believe it is time for new Lords of the Vale" ("The Pointy End"). In this conversation, Tyrion uses repetition to bring his point across more strongly and to manifest the idea that the Lords of the Vale look down upon the hill tribes and do not respect them. Furthermore, he establishes that he is siding with the hill tribes, creating an affinity between them by saying that the Lords of the Vale are his enemy. He thus infers that mutual enemies should make them allies.

---

[2] Tyrion demands a 'trial by combat' where two champions fight against each other, one representing the accuser and one representing the accused. If the champion of the accused wins, the accused is deemed innocent. Bronn volunteers to fight for Tyrion and wins the battle, which makes Tyrion an innocent man.

What is striking in this conversation between Tyrion and the hill tribes is the gap of social status, with Tyrion being one of the most noble people in Westeros and the hill tribes being among the lowest of people. Florian Coulmas claims that social status has an influence on the way people speak and which dialect and register they choose to use (62), and additionally, he refers to Peter Trudgill, who asserts that language is often accommodated in face-to-face situations by reducing dissimilarities in speech patterns (Coulmas 62). In order to make a conversation more reciprocal, these differences must be overcome so that both parties can adapt to a common level of speech.

Tyrion makes use of this strategy, actively seeking similarities between himself and the hill tribes, as little as they may be, in order to overcome this societal barrier. For instance, he knows not to mock the hill tribes and to address the tribe leaders with their appropriate names. By claiming that he also dislikes the Lords of the Vale, he fully manifests the similarities between himself and the tribes and manages to win them over. In the end, he not only manages to escape their attack and survive, but he also bribes them into fighting for his father's army. Again, this scene showcases Tyrion's quick wit and assessment of situations and his ability to adapt his style of speech to appeal to his opponents in a way that lets him come out of the situation with a favorable result.

It is notable to say in this case that, as much as Littlefinger used sexuality as another means of influence, Tyrion uses his family's name and the wealth that comes along with it. In both cases described above, he is able to persuade people by bribing them with money and lands, and he continues to do this throughout the entire series. Most evident is this in his relationship with the sellsword Bronn, who seems to be a friend but is ultimately only in it for the money and the prospect of titles and lands. This shows that Tyrion frequently uses gold to literally buy himself out of perilous situations. It is thus a combination of his wit and ability to adapt his speech to social settings and people of different identities along with his ability to promise wealth and status as a reward that lets him come out on top.

Finally, one of the prime examples of Tyrion's usage of speech in order to regain power is his second trial, where he is accused of murdering his nephew, King Joffrey. The trial, which is held by his father Tywin Lannister, who despises him, goes on for a while and various witnesses are brought forth, all of them testifying against Tyrion. It seems the trial is already decided, biased against Tyrion and he is aware that nothing he could say would sway his father to change his accusations and proclaim him innocent. Instead of accepting his fate, however, Tyrion again resolves to using a speech in order to regain control:

> "I did not kill Joffrey, but I wish that I had. Watching your vicious bastard die gave me more relief than a thousand lying whores. I wish I was the monster you think I am. I wish I had enough poison for the whole pack of you. I would gladly give my life to watch you all swallow it […]. I will not give my life for Joffrey's murder and I know I'll not get justice here, so I will let the Gods decide my fate. I demand a trial by combat." ("The Laws of Gods and Men")

He knows that his statements will not change the course of the trial, so he utters his true sentiments and showcases his resentment towards his father, his sister, and the lords and ladies who are witnessing the trial. This scene draws a parallel to the previous trial in the Vale of Arryn, where, as mentioned above, he was successful and walked away as a free man. In this case, he also has the upper hand in the trial, at least towards the end, surprising his father with his demand for a trial by combat. Yet, as it turns out in this case, his champion Oberyn Martell loses the combat, thus deeming Tyrion guilty.

Regardless of the outcome, what this speech indicates is that Tyrion possesses a great awareness of his counterparts and his audience, knowing that almost everyone in that room wants to see him dead. He uses this knowledge to expose the injustice of the trial and thus manages to momentarily gain control over the further development of the trial.

These examples highlight the fact that language usually needs to be adapted to the social setting and the identities of the conversational partners and that it is necessary to first eliminate great dissimilarities, such as the rudimental hill tribes vs. Tyrion as a noble person, in order to allow for a successful conversation. Tyrion is aware that he needs to adapt his way of speaking to the situation and he is quite savvy in ascertaining the identity of his opponents, using this to his advantage in order to persuade them to help him. With this strategy he not only manages to become a likeable character who is able to identify with the more lowborn and less advantaged characters but also to make sure he remains in a position of power.

IV

These brief analyses of some of Littlefinger's and Tyrion's dialogues illustrate the strength that language can play in gaining and maintaining power. It shows that Cersei's statement that only power yields power is not entirely correct and that there are certainly other ways of coming out on top. In Littlefinger's case, this includes the use of so-called 'mind control' or manipulation of characters into doing his bidding and, disregarding the moral complications of this, his technique is rather successful. Similarly, Tyrion finds his strength in wisdom and language, using his impeccable understanding of situations with ease and managing to talk his way out of any unfavorable situation he is met with, which allows him ultimately to survive the game surrounding the Iron Throne. He is so successful with his strategy that at the end of the series he ends up as Hand of the King on the Small Council, the second most powerful position in all of Westeros ("The Iron Throne").

This shows that language plays a larger role than initially expected and that knowledge, as an outcome of language usage, is of great value. In a world where power has so many different forms (status, wealth, even dragons!) anything that helps in order to secure a powerful position is important. And when you find yourself in a world where, as Cersei states, "you win or you die", it is of utmost importance to find a way to actually win, because winning means survival. Tyrion finds himself in so many seemingly hopeless situations where the result could have been his death, but he battles that death sentence with his wits and wisdom. Littlefinger, on the other hand, never even faces a mortally critical situation (up until his demise) because he acts in the shadows of others, being the silent manipulator and letting others take the blame for his game.

Admittedly, as briefly put forward above, there are other factors that also contribute to Littlefinger's and Tyrion's rise to power, and language should always be seen as a result of various social and personal elements that interact with each other. With so many different characters involved and events happening at once, it is difficult to pinpoint the exact recipe for power, but as the examples of Tyrion and Littlefinger have shown, the right use of language and speech can be beneficial to one's own desires and can help manifest a certain amount of power.

Littlefinger and Tyrion have thus been surprisingly successful in reaching power, despite their obvious physical and societal disadvantages, and they outlive many of the more traditionally powerful people who have had a quick rise but an even quicker fall such as Robert Baratheon, Stannis Baratheon, Robb Stark and Joffrey Baratheon. This goes to show that there is more to power than strength and status, that different factors weave into each other and that, as Littlefinger suggests, one must always be one or more steps ahead of the others in order to survive.

Bibliography

"A Golden Crown." *Game of Thrones Season 1*, written by David Benioff and D.B. Weiss, directed by Daniel Minahan, HBO, 2012. DVD.

Coulmas, Florian. "The Power to Choose and Its Sociolinguistic Implications." *Along the Routes to Power: Explorations of Empowerment through Language.* Ed. Martin Pütz, Joshua A. Fishman and JoAnne Neff-van Aertselaer. De Gruyter, 2006, 55-71.

"Cripples, Bastards, and Broken Things." *Game of Thrones Season 1*, written by David Benioff and D.B. Weiss, directed by Brian Kirk, HBO, 2012. DVD.

Edwards, John. "The Power of Language, the Language of Power." *Along the Routes to Power: Explorations of Empowerment through Language.* Ed. Martin Pütz, Joshua A. Fishman, JoAnne Neff-van Aertselaer. De Gruyter, 2006, 13-34.

Fairclough, Norman. *Language and Power.* Pearson Education Limited, 2001.

"First of His Name." *Game of Thrones Season 4*, written by David Benioff and D.B. Weiss, directed by Michelle MacLaren, HBO 2015. DVD.

"Lord Snow." *Game of Thrones Season 1,* written by David Benioff and D.B. Weiss, directed by Brian Kirk, HBO, 2012. DVD.

Savage-Rumbaugh, Sue, William Mintz Fields and Jared Taglialatela. "Ape Consciousness-Human Consciousness: A Perspective Informed by Language and Culture." *American Zoologist*, 40.6 (2000): 910-921.

Schneck, Stephen Frederick. "Michel Foucault on Power/ Discourse, Theory and Practice." *Human Studies. Foucault Memorial Issue*, 10.1 (1987): 15-33.

"The Climb." *Game of Thrones Season 3,* written by David Benioff and D.B. Weiss, directed by Alik Sakharov, HBO, 2014. DVD.

"The Iron Throne." *Game of Thrones Season 8,* written by David Benioff and D.B. Weiss, directed by David Benioff and D.B. Weiss, HBO, 2019. Sky on Demand.

"The Kingsroad." *Game of Thrones Season 1,* written by David Benioff and D.B. Weiss, directed by Timothy van Patten, HBO, 2012. DVD.

"The Laws of Gods and Men." *Game of Thrones Season 4,* written by Bryan Cogman, directed by Alik Sakharov, HBO, 2015. DVD.

"The North Remembers." *Game of Thrones Season 2,* written by David Benioff and D.B. Weiss, directed by Alan Taylor, HBO, 2013. DVD.

"The Pointy End." *Game of Thrones Season 1,* written by George R.R. Martin, directed by Daniel Minahan, HBO, 2012. DVD.

"The Queen's Justice." *Game of Thrones Season 7,* written by David Benioff and D.B. Weiss, directed by Mark Mylod, HBO, 2017. DVD.

Tveten, John, and Gloria Tveten. *Our Life with Birds. A Nature Trails Book.* Texas A&M University Press, 2004.

van Dijk, Teun A. *Discourse and Power.* Palgrave Macmillan, 2008.

Weber, Max. *Economy and Society: An Outline of Interpretive Sociology.* Ed. Günther Roth and Claus Wittich. University of California Press, 1978.

"What Is Dead May Never Die." *Game of Thrones Season 2,* written by Bryan Cogman, directed by Alik Sakharov, HBO, 2013. DVD.

"Winter Is Coming." *Game of Thrones Season 1*, written by David Benioff and D.B. Weiss, directed by Timothy van Patten, HBO, 2012. DVD.

Die Autorinnen und Autoren

Elin Fredsted hat an der Aarhus Universitet (DK) Nordistik und Germanistik studiert. Ph.d. in Sprachwissenschaft 1996. 1979-1983 Lektorin für Dänisch an der CAU Kiel. 1984-1990 freiberufliche Tätigkeit als bidirektionale Dolmetscherin, 1990-2000 in verschiedenen Funktionen an Forschungsinstitutionen und Universitäten in Dänemark tätig, zuletzt als associate professor an der Syddansk Universitet (DK). 2000-2019 Professorin für dänische Sprache und Literatur an der Europa-Universität Flensburg. 2014 Mitbegründerin und erste Direktorin des Zentrums für kleine und regionale Sprachen. Erhielt 2017 den Forschungspreis der Europa-Universität Flensburg. Forschungsschwerpunkte: Sprachkontakt und Mehrsprachigkeit.

Marie Hartkopf is a prospective PhD student in American Studies at the Europa-Universität Flensburg, where she also completed a Master's degree in 'Culture, Language and Media' with a focus on American literature and film. Prior to her Master's degree, she has studied Educational Sciences at the same university with the subjects English and Health and Nutrition. She is an avid researcher and writer, interested in a variety of topics ranging from Afro-American culture to fantasy and science-fiction to astrophysics and future technologies. In her free time, she finds balance through yoga and works on writing young adult and science-fiction stories, with the intention of eventually publishing a novel.

Janice L. Jake is Chair of the English Department at Midlands Technical College in Columbia, SC. Her research interests lie in language contact, especially codeswitching. Dr. Jake's research focuses on extending the principles of the Matrix Language Frame Model (Myers-Scotton, *Duelling Languages*, 1993) and the 4-M Model of morpheme classification (Jake and Myers-Scotton, "The 4-M model: Different routes in production for different morphemes," Adamou and Matras, eds., in press) to other contact phenomena, such as language acquisition (Jake, "Constructing Interlanguage," Linguistics 36(2), 1998), pidgin and creole linguistics, and the intersection of socio- and psycholinguistics in contact phenomena (Myers-Scotton and Jake, "Cross-linguistic asymmetries in code-switching patterns: implications for bilingual language production," 2015, in Schwieter, ed.).

Alexander Jöckel: Diplom Ingenieur (FH) der Elektro- und Informationstechnik, mit dem Schwerpunkt Automation und Robotik, hat an der Hochschule Fulda studiert. Seit 2007 in der Forschung und Entwicklung, auf den Gebieten der Digitalen Fabrik und Industrieautomation, sowie Automotive-, Consumer- und Medizinelektronik. Seit Frühjahr 2020 als ein Hardwareentwickler für Funktionale Sicherheit tätig, der Abteilung Smart Infrastructure bei der Siemens AG.

Shiva Leicht studiert Kultur – Sprache – Medien an der Europa Universität-Flensburg und ist begeisterte Comicleserin und Science Fiction-Fan. Geboren in Flensburg und aufgewachsen zwischen Nord- und Ostsee, Dänemark und Deutschland, fühlt sie sich als Grenzgängerin und Grenzen-Sprengerin.

Bruce Martin is Program Director of Computer Technology at Midlands Technical College in Columbia, SC. His primary research interests lie in the intersection of computer science and linguistics; his Ph.D. dissertation explores the analysis of ambiguity in expressions and their interpretation. In his work, he examines the limits of neural networks in artificial intelligence. Dr. Martin is also involved in developing standards in computer science education for secondary schools in the state of South Carolina.

Markus Pohlmeyer: Dichter, Essayist und Autor bei CulturMag/ CrimeMag, lehrt an der Europa Universität-Flensburg Katholische Theologie und im Studiengang Kultur-Sprache-Medien.

Flensburger Studien zu Literatur und Theologie

Band 1
Markus Pohlmeyer: Science Fiction – Filmisch-literarisches Exil
des Göttlichen, Br., 140 Seiten, 19,50 €, ISBN 978-3-86815-587-7,
2., durchgesehene Auflage, Igel Verlag, Hamburg 2014.

Band 2
Markus Pohlmeyer: Cult(ur)mix. Religiöse Phänomene in Comics
und TV-Serien, Br., 100 Seiten, 19,50 €, ISBN 978-3-86815-702-4,
Igel Verlag, Hamburg 2015.

Band 3
Marcello Neri / Markus Pohlmeyer (Hg.): Zwischen Welten verstrickt.
Gedanken zu Europa, Religion und Literatur, Br., 144 Seiten, 19,50 €,
ISBN 978-3-86815-703-1, Igel Verlag, Hamburg 2015.

Band 4
Markus Pohlmeyer (Hg.): Kierkegaard – eine Schlüsselfigur
der europäischen Moderne, Br., 244 Seiten, 34,90 €,
ISBN 978-3-86815-704-8, Igel Verlag, Hamburg 2015.

Band 5
Markus Pohlmeyer: Als ich zu den Sternen ging. Gedichte,
Br., 108 Seiten, 19,50 €, ISBN 978-3-86815-708-6, Igel Verlag,
Hamburg 2016.

Band 6
Markus Pohlmeyer: Zwischen Welten verstrickt II.
Essays zu (pop)kulturellen Phänomenen, Br., 104 Seiten, 19,50 €,
ISBN 978-3-86815-709-3, Igel Verlag, Hamburg 2016.

Band 7
Markus Pohlmeyer (Hg.): Cult(ur)mix II.
Fragment – Unschärfe – Labyrinth: auf dem Weg zu einer
popkulturellen Anthropologie, Br., 164 Seiten, 19,50 €,
ISBN 978-3-86815-711-6, Igel Verlag, Hamburg 2016.

Band 8
Markus Pohlmeyer (Hg.): Töchter der Sonne. Eine Inka-Kantate.
Gedichte. Mit einem Kompositionsbericht von A. N. Tarkmann und
alt-amerikanistischen Erläuterungen von B. Schmelz, Br., 88 Seiten,
16,90 €, ISBN 978-3-86815-712-3, 2., überarbeitete Auflage 2017,
Igel Verlag, Hamburg 2017.

Band 9
Elin Fredsted / Markus Pohlmeyer (Hg.): Zwischen Welten
verstrickt III. Filmanalysen: Zwischen Heimat und Science Fiction,
Mit Beiträgen von J. Jake und A. Jöckel, Br., 96 Seiten, 19,50 €,
ISBN 978-3-86815-723-9, Igel Verlag, Hamburg 2017.

Band 10
Markus Pohlmeyer: Zwischen Welten verstrickt IV. Weltraum,
Wildwest und allerlei wunderliche Wege, Br., 108 Seiten, 19,50 €,
ISBN 978-3-86815-724-6, Igel Verlag, Hamburg 2017.

Band 11
Markus Pohlmeyer / Bernd Schmelz (Hg.): Weihnachten.
Von der globalisierten Postmoderne in die Antike – (un)gewohnte
Zugänge, Br., 140 Seiten, 19,50 €, ISBN 978-3-86815-725-3,
Igel Verlag, Hamburg 2017.

Band 12
Markus Pohlmeyer: Als ich zu den Sternen ging. Zweiter Teil.
Gedichte, Br., 112 Seiten, 19,50 €, ISBN 978-3-86815-728-4,
Igel Verlag, Hamburg 2018.

Band 13
Markus Pohlmeyer: Dinosaurier, kosmische Träumer und Minihelden.
Zwischen Welten verstrickt V, Br., 108 Seiten, 19,50 €,
ISBN 978-3-86815-731-4, Igel Verlag, Hamburg 2018.

Band 14

Benny Grey Schuster: Das Osterlachen. Darstellung der Kulturgeschichte und Theologie des Osterlachens sowie ein Essay über die kulturelle, kirchliche und theologische Verwandlung des Lachens. Aus dem Dänischen übersetzt von Eberhard Harbsmeier, Br., 428 Seiten, 44,00 €, ISBN 978-3-86815-731-4, Igel Verlag, Hamburg 2019.

Band 15

Markus Pohlmeyer / Christian Stolz (Hg.): Ostern – Ursprünge und Bräuche, Br., 136 Seiten, 22,00 €, ISBN 978-3-86815-734-5, Igel Verlag, Hamburg 2019.

Band 16

Elin Fredsted / Markus Pohlmeyer (Hg.): Heimat: kulturwissenschaftliche, regionalgeschichtliche und ästhetische Zugänge, Br., 144 Seiten, 22,00 €, ISBN 978-3-86815-735-2, Igel Verlag, Hamburg 2019.

Band 17

Franz Januschek / Markus Pohlmeyer (Hg.): Zeitreise. Transzendenz im Science Fiction-Format, Br., 144 Seiten, 22,00 €, ISBN 978-3-86815-735-2, Igel Verlag, Hamburg 2019.

Band 18

Markus Pohlmeyer: Schöpfungen: Science Fiction, Comic, Western. Von Platon bis Cixin Liu. Zwischen Welten verstrickt VI, Br., 124 Seiten, 19,50 €, ISBN 978-3-86815-739-0, Igel Verlag, Hamburg 2019.